Doing It
GOD'S Way

From Conflict to Harmony
in Church Leadership

Doing It
GOD'S
Way

From Conflict to Harmony in Church Leadership

by

PAUL CANNINGS, PhD

URIEL PRESS

All Bible references and quotes are from the following Bible
versions: New American Standard, Amplified, King James
Version, The Message, and New Living Translation.

Published in the United States by Uriel Press, a division of UMI
P.O. Box 436987, Chicago, IL 60643
www.urielpress.com

ISBN: 978-0-9993326-6-5 (paperback)
ISBN: 978-0-9993326-7-2 (eBook)

Cover design: Laura Duffy
Book design: Astrid Lewis Reedy

For more information about speaking engagements with Pastor
Paul Cannings or to order multiple copies of this title, please
contact Power Walk Ministries at www.powerwalkministries.org.

Printed in the United States of America

Dedication

I dedicate this book to the call for leadership whether it is in the church or the home. Growing up in a home that taught and projected the need to submit to the Lordship of Christ out of a love for His Word taught me the benefits of Christian leadership. Whether it was the early morning devotions led by my mother or the Sunday devotions led by my father, the elders who led the church, or the youth minister who led our youth group, I came to understand and appreciate the need for godly leadership. As a result, I must first dedicate this book to my parents, James Basil and Annie Ellen Cannings.

I also thank God for my wife, Everette Cannings, who out of our love for God and her family, has been God's powerful instrument in sharing the development of our two sons Paul Jr. and Pierre. Our sons have blessed us with seven grandchildren (Paul III, Nathalia, Tylia, Everson, Cholie, Carter, and Kyla) as a result of their marriages to Tanisha and Monica, respectively. We have been truly blessed.

Thanks be to God for His AMAZING GRACE!

Table of Contents

❖ ACKNOWLEDGMENTS

In 1969, as a result of the influence of my parents and my mother's morning devotions that took place every school day morning, I accepted Christ into my life during a church service in Guyana, South America. This moment in time was and is the greatest event in my life. I would like to thank the Lord God, who sought me and drew me to Himself, for loving me so much that He would allow me to be a part of His eternal family.

My wife, Everette, has been an avid supporter in all aspects of my life since our friendship began in 1979 extending into our marriage on September 6, 1980. I give her my deep gratitude for all her years of sacrifice and encouragement, which has allowed me to remain focused. She has blessed my life in so many ways. Our sons, Paul Jr. and Pierre, and their wives, Tanisha and Monica, respectively, are also a blessing. I am blessed to witness their love for the Lord and to each other. When I see their families, my heart is strengthened and renewed. I thought that this would always be the delight of my life until my wife and I were provided from their marriages seven grandchildren: Paul III, Natalia, Tylia, Everson, Cholie, Carter, and Kyla. Our grandchildren became the greatest joys of our lives. I praise the Lord for allowing my wife and me to experience such joy.

I also thank my Administrative Assistant Gail O'Neal for all the work it takes to make so many things possible. Her tireless commitment to see the Lord's work make a difference in people's lives is truly a blessing. It is because of the staff at Living Word Fellowship Church serving the Lord faithfully that I am able to find the time to make this material available.

Special thanks to Miriam Glover for her insight, hard work, and commitment to see this book through to the end. She has edited this work, proofread through much material, and has helped the vision become a reality, as the Lord has ordained.

Special thanks also to Pastor Earl Lewis and Pastor Lee Skinner for their commitment to Power Walk Ministries. They have been faithful board members and are committed servants of God. They have made many sacrifices that have blessed this ministry to progress, and it has not gone unnoticed.

I cannot help but thank God for calling me to serve Him. There have been many difficult days, but each experience has taught me more, has strengthened my resolve, and has caused me to fall more deeply in love with Him. Growing in my relationship with the Lord has been one of the most challenging life experiences I have had, but it has been the single greatest empowering journey of my life.

I thank God for calling me to pastor Living Word Fellowship Church. I thank Him because it has driven me to desire to learn more about the Lord, to draw closer and closer to Him so that I can be what He wants me to be for His people. I love the people the Lord has called for me to serve because of their desire to know Christ and to make Him known. We have shared a lot together as a church family and it has blessed us to experience God more deeply as we learn to trust Him more.

I always find it interesting that the Bible begins with God taking the initiative to lead the development of earth for His glory (Revelation 4:11) and for the extension of the Godhead's relationship to mankind (Genesis 1:26-28). His entire plan is extended through Christ (Colossians 1:15-18) who is the 'Alpha and the Omega' all of it (Revelation 1:8; 21:6; 22:13). God did not and does not ask for anyone's ideas; *"Having made known unto us the mystery of his will, according to his good pleasure which he hath purposed in himself...."* (Ephesians 1:9-10) It is the lack of leadership demonstrated in Adam that led to chaos for all mankind (Romans 5:15). Again, it is the leadership of God that allows for mankind to be redeemed (John 3:16; 2 Corinthians 3:18).

Leadership is best seen through the eyes of God whether a person is a pastor (all scripture is given by inspiration of God, and is profitable for doctrine, for reproof, for correction, for instruction in righteousness: That the man of God may be perfect, thoroughly furnished unto all good works; 2 Timothy 3:16-17) or a person is seeking to work out their salvation in fear and trembling (Philippians 2:12-13; 2 Peter 1:3-4). It is when a man submits to being Christ and his wife commits to being the church that marriage is at its best (Ephesians 5:32) and children can be raised to multiply the image of God as originally designed (Ephesians 6:1-4). This kind of leadership inspired by God is wholesome with eternal ramifications.

It is when leaders submit to the Lordship of Christ that leadership is most effective. We see this demonstrated when Moses cries out to

God for help in Numbers 11:10-15. God's reply was *"And the Lord said unto Moses, Gather unto me seventy men of the elders of Israel, whom thou knowest to be the elders of the people, and officers over them; and bring them unto the tabernacle of the congregation, that they may stand there with thee. And I will come down and talk with thee there: and I will take of the spirit which is upon thee, and will put it upon them; and they shall bear the burden of the people with thee, that thou bear it not thyself alone."* (Numbers 11:16-17)

Similarly, when Joshua is called to lead God said to him: *"Only be thou strong and very courageous, that thou mayest observe to do according to all the law, which Moses my servant commanded thee: turn not from it to the right hand or to the left, that thou mayest prosper whithersoever thou goest. This book of the law shall not depart out of thy mouth; but thou shalt meditate therein day and night, that thou mayest observe to do according to all that is written therein: for then thou shalt make thy way prosperous, and then thou shalt have good success."* (Joshua 1:7-8)

The same takes place when the apostles and elders needed to come to an agreement concerning the Apostle Paul going to the Gentiles. Christ chose to speak to Peter on the rooftop in order to send him to Cornelius' house so that Peter would understand that there is no difference between Jew and Gentile (Acts 1:24-35). This revelation opened the eyes of the apostles and elders so that they came to a resolution in Acts 15. It is when the church does not submit to the Lordship of Christ His lampstand is removed from the church and the church becomes void (Revelation 2-3). Moses' submission to the Lordship of God causes Israel to be led to the Promised Land or, in the case of Nehemiah, a wall is rebuilt for the obedient people who returned to the Promised Land. Leaders who are led by God are the most powerful and productive men and women who blessed God's eternal purposes.

Sometimes we lead because it is requested of us and we feel a sense of responsibility. We must change that outlook. We must see leadership as a need to carry out God's plan for mankind not just to save mankind so that each person goes to heaven; we must see it as a need to bring heaven on earth so that the glory of God is manifested vividly to the world. *"Thou art worthy, O Lord, to receive glory and honour and power: for thou hast created all things, and for thy pleasure they are and were created."* (Revelation 4:11) Paul puts it this way: *"And whatsoever ye do in word or deed, do all in the name of the Lord Jesus, giving thanks to God and the Father by him."* (Colossians 3:17)

When this focus drives us, it is going to be the focus that unites us. It is when we understand we have one common enemy and one purpose (Philippians 2:1-2), whatever divides us must be addressed so that united we can resist the attacks of Satan for the legacy God has gifted us to provide.

In talking to my brother one day (a retired military tank sergeant), who was in many military campaigns, he said that he did not first fight for his country; he first fought for the man next to him. *"Let nothing be done through strife or vainglory, but in lowliness of mind let each esteem other better than themselves. Look not every man on his own things, but every man also on the things of others. Let this mind be in you, which was also in Christ Jesus: Who, being in the form of God, thought it not robbery to be equal with God: But made himself of no reputation, and took upon him the form of a servant, and was made in the likeness of men: And being found in fashion as a man, he humbled himself, and became obedient unto death, even the death of the cross. Wherefore God also hath highly exalted him and given him a name which is above every name: That at the name of Jesus every knee should bow, of things in heaven, and things in earth, and things under the earth; And that every tongue should confess that Jesus Christ is Lord, to the glory of God the Father."* (Philippians 2:3-11)

When it is all about God, we selflessly build a lasting legacy (1 Corinthians 15:58). When we lead for our own purposes, we may develop something great in the eyes of men, but as Revelation 3:1-6 explains, it would not have the transformation that blesses homes, churches, communities, and countries eternally for God's glory because Christ eventually removes His lampstand. 1 Corinthians 3:10-15 says that if it is 'gold, silver, precious stones, wood, hay, straw' there is no eternal reward. So it is always best to lead united for the purposes of God.

It is because of what is at stake, especially in a world that God says is going to get worse, that leadership for God's purposes is important and remaining united for His glory is essential. This is the inspiration behind this book. Throughout the over thirty years of ministry, this is what makes or breaks a church or a home. This is what determines if a nation is strong or weak. If leadership is absent from the home, what is to come is unimaginable. *"And he shall turn the heart of the fathers to the children, and the heart of the children to their fathers, lest I come and smite the earth with a curse."* (Malachi 4:6; KJV) As the world drifts more and more away from God, believers' love for God can grow cold (Matthew 24:9-24). Leadership is not just important; it is significant to God's plan expanding for His glory.

CHAPTER 1

Principles for Developing a United Leadership Team

Introduction

The absolute foundation for developing church ministry must rest on the authority of the Word of God. Leaders are, therefore, guided and directed as a result of the principles outlined in scripture. Because Christ is the head of the church (Ephesians 1:22), leaders must function under His headship, in order to facilitate God's plans, purpose, and will for the church (Ephesians 1:11). Leaders do not have to develop principles by which to guide the church; these principles are already outlined, and they stand as the authority for God's church (2 Timothy 3:14-17; take notice of 'every good work' mentioned in verse 17).

It is a commitment to His standards that leads to unity. Unity is achieved when the Word of God defines the purpose of ministry (one Word), people are challenged to mature spiritually (one Spirit), each person is committed to use their spiritual gift for the glory of God (1 Corinthians 12:4-8; which leads to one body), and each person is committed to one purpose (Philippians 2:1-5). As Christ prepared His disciples for His departure, He prayed for the church to function as a unified body (John 17:20-23).

When these elements lead to unity, diversity serves to make a unified body a powerful experience that accomplishes God's purposes with a high level of efficiency. *"There is one body and one Spirit, just as also you were called in one hope of your calling; one Lord, one faith, one baptism, one God and Father of all who is over all and through all and in all. But to each one of us grace was given according to the measure of Christ's gift."* (Ephesians 4:4-7)

A Biblical Process that Empowers Church Leadership to Minister as a Team

Leaders Must Address Divisive Behavior Biblically

1. Leaders must not tolerate members who seek to create division in the church. These passages instruct leadership to do the following:

   a. *"Keep an eye on those who cause dissension and hindrances..."* (Romans 16:17).

   b. *"Take special note ... and do not associate with him ... admonish him as a brother."* (2 Thessalonians 3:14-15).

   c. When a person persists in creating dissension, we must do the following:

   "...avoid foolish controversies and genealogies and strife and disputes about the law, ... Reject a factious man after a first and second warning..." (Titus 3:10).

2. Leaders must be more <u>committed to the Word of God</u> rather than <u>traditions</u> (Colossians 2:6-8; Mark 7:5-8). In other words, when church members are more committed to the church's traditions (later chapter) than living out the principles of the Word, the traditions must be removed so that the church remains a living organism (Hebrews 10:23-26) rather than a stiff, religious institution.

3. Leaders must not <u>be argumentative</u> (1 Timothy 6:3-5; 2 Timothy 2:14, 24; Proverbs 17:19).

    a. *"For the overseer must be above reproach as God's steward, <u>not self-willed</u>, not quick-tempered, not addicted to wine, not pugnacious, not fond of sordid gain...."* (Titus 1:7; NASB) It is not about winning an argument. It is about executing the will of the Lord for the spiritual development of His people (Colossians 1:28-29). Jesus constantly stated, no matter the arguments of the High Priest, Elders, Pharisees, or Scribes, He 'must be about His Father's business.'

A Process for Establishing a Cohesive Leadership Team

1. Each leader must function based on their spiritual gifts (Romans 12:4-13; 1 Peter 4:10). This provides the spiritual empowerment necessary to fulfill the will of God. In other words, an elder should not be considered an elder if they do not have the gift of wisdom and knowledge (Jeremiah 3:15). A deacon should not be considered to be a deacon if they do not have the gift of service (Acts 6:2-3). A Sunday school teacher should not teach if they do not have the gift of teaching.

2. The leadership team must serve <u>based on the vision</u> of the church (Philippians 2:1-2).

3. They also must serve committed to respect <u>pastoral leadership</u> (Exodus 18:19-20; Numbers 11:16-18; Titus 2:15; 1 Timothy 3:15).

    a. Providing respect to a key leader maintains unity to a vision and the work that needs to be done to execute the vision. It stimulates spiritual growth which leads to a loving community of believers (Ephesians 4:12-13,16).

4. They must learn to <u>respect differences</u> (Romans 14) and function compelled to exercise God's love to each other. Must <u>respect structure</u> when there are differences so that those issues are resolute

with decency and order (1 Corinthians 14:33, 40). *Discussed in chapter two.

5. Organize a structure based on the ministry's vision that defines how each person works as a team based on their spiritual gift (1 Corinthians 12:14-27).

6. Seek to function without grumbling and complaining (Philippians 2:14; 1 Peter 4:7-11; 1 Corinthians 10:10; Colossians 3:13). Only entertain constructive criticism. Discussed in chapter three.

The Spirit of a Leader Determines the Overall Effectiveness of the Leadership Team

1. Christian leaders are servants: (Matthew 20:27, 28; Mark 10:44, 45). "Leaders in the church exist to facilitate the ministry of the whole body; they are not appointed to dominate or control the body." (James E. Means, page 47) Discussed in chapter seven.

2. Single-mindedness (outlined by Jay Adams. "Be the Leader God Meant You to Be"):

   a. The Apostle Paul said, "I press toward the mark." He did not say, "I float toward the mark, I glide toward the mark, I slip and slide toward the mark, or I drift toward the mark." He said press, and that always presupposes opposition. (Romans 1:16-18; 1 Corinthians 16:9; Philippians 4:12; 1 Timothy 4:6-8; Colossians 1:29)

   Today the Lord is looking for people who care nothing for the empty praise or temporal pleasures of this world (1 John 2:15-17). He is seeking men and women who care that the world needs Christ and who are eager to follow Him with single-mindedness and purpose (Colossians 3:1-3; Acts 20:24).

3. A leader that will be effective must be flexible (1 Corinthians 16:6-7; 2 Corinthians 1:15-17; Acts 16:6).

4. A leader who does not <u>run from challenges</u> (1 Corinthians 16:9; 2 Corinthians 4:10), does not quit leaving the group incapacitated.

Barriers that Prevent People from Working Together

1. When a leader becomes more focused on obstacles rather than developing effective strategies for the achievement of the group's objectives, the group becomes easily caught up in resolving one problem after another. This reduces productivity and increases frustration (1 Kings 19 – Elijah can take on many obstacles, but Jezebel was too much, so he kept hiding from her).

2. When leaders don't trust leadership, they begin to do what they think is best. This leads to a dysfunctional and divisive environment. It is better for the person to resign (Numbers 13-14, 16).

3. A lack of clearly <u>defined goals and objectives</u> (Philippians 2:1-2; one purpose and one mind).

4. Leaders who do things last minute. This does not allow for <u>good communication and team building</u>.

5. Leaders who are unwilling to try anything new that the Word of God allows (Mark 7:5-8).

6. Leaders that are <u>not teachable</u> (2 Timothy 2:2).

7. Leaders who have too <u>much self-confidence</u> (Matthew 16:21-23; 1 Peter 5:5).

8. Leaders whose <u>secular education</u> leads to over-confidence and a lack of dependence on God for Christian ministry (2 Corinthians 3:4-6).

9. Barriers occur when there is no clear line of command and there is a lack of structure.

10. When committee members are <u>carnal Christians,</u> there are a lot of

barriers (1 Corinthians 3:1-3). People functioning in the flesh can create a lot of chaos in a church (Galatians 5:16-21).

11. This takes place when everything is being done based on leaders' opinions, their need for power and authority, their need for a sense of security, and when leaders have their own best interests ahead of what the Word says, both conceptually (2 Timothy 3:17) and in action.

12. A lack of accountability or individuals not wanting to be accountable reduces the effectiveness of any group.

Group Dynamics That Can Lead to a Cohesive Group of Believers

There are several stages in developing cohesive group dynamics. They are as follows:

1. Getting to know each other through fellowship gatherings. Don't just meet to accomplish tasks. This can develop good communication among the leadership team and reduce competition.

2. Everyone working based on their spiritual gifts.

3. Make sure everyone has a clear understanding of the task.

4. Make sure everyone has a good understanding of the vision of the church and how it is systematically implemented in a strategic plan.

5. Developing a level of confidence in the leader.

6. Each ministry leader must be provided clear ministry guidelines (another way of saying that each person has a job description) that complements what others are doing.

7. A leader needs to always think positively and remain excited about the project. This encourages a workable attitude among members.

8. Develop confidence in the ability of each member of the committee.

9. Respect difference so long as it does not take away from the overall objectives.

10. Develop a <u>level of commitment</u> to the accomplishment of the task.

11. Divide the <u>overall task into parts</u> so that the group feels a sense of accomplishment from time to time.

12. Practice good <u>problem-solving techniques</u>.

13. <u>Compliment people</u> when the opportunity arises.

14. Seek to develop <u>good communication</u> within the group.

Conclusion

Unity is not uniformity. Unity is created a lot easier when believers sincerely love the Lord because they will keep His commandments (Matthew 22:36-40). The Word teaches that once someone truly loves God His love becomes complete and they develop a natural tendency to love others (Matthew 22:37-40; 1 John 2:3-6; 4-12). When believers are more focused on the task and not on their own spiritual development, believers soon begin to function in their own flesh which only leads to strife and dissension.

It is not that we do not need to develop the skills necessary to do ministry. It is that these skills are useless to the productive development of God's kingdom work when they are not empowered by the Spirit of God (1 Peter 4:10). Christ told His disciples that if they do not abide in Him they can do nothing (John 15:3-5). Paul continues this thought by telling us we are inadequate to do ministry without being equipped by the comprehensive Word of God (2 Corinthians 3:4-6; 2 Timothy 3:17; 2 Peter 1:3-4). *"...So that the man of God may be adequate, equipped for every good work."* (2 Timothy 3:17)

CHAPTER 2

United as One in Ministry: Managing Conflicts Biblically

Introduction

One of the scenarios that takes place throughout scripture is conflict. It begins with Cain and Abel and continues even to Christ and Peter in Matthew 16:21-23. Paul going to the Gentiles created a great dispute (Acts 15:1-35). Paul and Barnabas had a dispute about John Mark (Acts 15:36-41); many preachers seem to speak against Paul's ministry (Philippians 1:15-18). Paul ends his ministry by telling Timothy who to look out for in 2 Timothy 4:9 and all those who turned on him in chapter 4:16-18.

The leaders of Acts 15, Paul and Barnabas (Acts 15:36-41) were all great men of God. They just disagreed. In the midst of all of this we see that because they were open to growing spiritually, many of these circumstances led to productive results. Here is an example, *"Aristarchus, my fellow prisoner, sends you his greetings; <u>and also Barnabas's cousin Mark</u> (about whom you received instructions; if he comes to you, welcome him); and also Jesus who is called Justus; these are the only fellow workers for the kingdom of God who are from the circumcision, and they have proved to be an encouragement to me."* (Colossians 4:10-12)

The Biblical Importance of Resolving Conflicts

A.   Christ's greatest desire for the church is that we must dwell in unity

(John 17:20-23), and we must keep Satan out (Matthew 16:17-19; Ephesians 3:10) by remaining accountable for our walk with God. This is important for the following reasons:

1. The church accomplishes its greatest need and that is to love others (1 Corinthians 13:3; 1 John 3:16-22).

2. Our oneness will be representative of the oneness of the Godhead. This means that even though there are differences (diverse spiritual gifts, differences in personalities and backgrounds), oneness can be achieved (John 17:22) because the Spirit of God lives in us all and the Word of God does not take sides.

3. The goal to make disciples has, for the most part, been accomplished by the love demonstrated among believers (John 13:34-35). This is very important to resolve conflict because discipleship develops a willingness to submit to the authority of Christ as directed by His Word (John 15:8-10; upcoming chapter).

4. In John 17:23, Christ says that when believers dwell in unity, the world comes to know that Christ lives.

5. If there is no love in the church, then Christ will no longer choose to abide there (Revelation 2:4-5).

B. Division and conflicts can hinder believers' prayers and worship before God (Matthew 5:22-24; John 15:8-9; 1 John 3:16-24).

C. Unresolved conflict in marriage that causes a husband not to live with his wife in an understanding manner can cause prayers to be hindered (1 Peter 3:7).

D. It is because of His Word and the work of the Holy Spirit in our lives we can be one despite our differences. *"…whereas our more presentable members have no need of it. But God has so composed the body, giving more abundant honor to that member which lacked, so that there may be no division in the body, but that the members may have the same care for one another. And if one member suffers, all the members suffer with it; if one member is honored, all the members rejoice with it."* (1 Corinthians 12:24-26)

E. When Jesus was asked, "What is the greatest commandment?", His response was awesome:

"And He said to him, 'YOU SHALL LOVE THE LORD YOUR GOD WITH ALL YOUR HEART, AND WITH ALL YOUR SOUL, AND WITH ALL YOUR MIND.' This is the great and foremost commandment. The second is like it, 'YOU SHALL LOVE YOUR NEIGHBOR AS YOURSELF.' On these two commandments depend the whole Law and the Prophets." (Matthew 22:37-40).

The Biblical Responsibility of the Church Believers for Resolving Conflict

A. Each member is commanded Biblically to respect the opinions of other believers (Anything that does not violate God's Word; Romans 14:1-10).

B. We must do whatever it takes not to be a stumbling block to one another (Romans 14:13,19; 1 Corinthians 8).

C. We must relate to one another without grumbling and complaining (Philippians 2:14; 1 Peter 4:7-11; 1 Corinthians 10:10; Colossians 3:12-15).

D. If they do not forgive one another God will not forgive them (Matthew 6:14-15):

  1. Forgiveness is not forgetting. We will remember what has transpired. Forgiveness is submitting to the Word of God as a guide for loving one another no matter the past.

     a. *"Do not grieve the Holy Spirit of God, by whom you were sealed for the day of redemption. Let all bitterness and wrath and anger and clamor and slander be put away from you, along with all malice. Be kind to one another, tender-hearted, forgiving each other, just as God in Christ also has forgiven you."* (Ephesians 4:30-32)

E. Anytime members see conflict creating division in the church, <u>they are commanded to address it</u> (Romans 16:17-20; 1 Thessalonians 5:14; 2 Thessalonians 3:10-13). <u>This is explained in chapter 1.</u>

The Biblical Responsibility of Church Leaders for Resolving Conflict

A. When leaders challenge the members of the church to serve, each member grows into the fullness of Christ (Ephesians 4:12-16). This process occurs:

1. If members submit to the equipping process, the church could serve <u>to restore whatever was broken</u> in the life of the believer (Galatians 6:1-5). As a result, the believer who is now functioning healthily blesses the church and the home (Ephesians 5:25-27, 32).

   a. *"And do not get drunk with wine, for that is dissipation, but be filled with the Spirit, speaking to one another in psalms and hymns and spiritual songs, singing and making melody with your heart to the Lord; always giving thanks for all things in the name of our Lord Jesus Christ to God, even the Father; and be subject to one another in the fear of Christ."* (Ephesians 5:17-21)

B. Paul instructed pastors to function in this manner:

1. *"If anyone advocates a different doctrine and does not agree with sound words, those of our Lord Jesus Christ, and with the doctrine conforming to godliness, he is conceited and understands nothing; but he has a morbid interest in controversial questions and disputes about words, out of which arise envy, strife, abusive language, evil suspicions, and constant friction between men of depraved mind and deprived of the truth, who suppose that godliness is a means of*

gain. But godliness actually is a means of great gain when accompanied by contentment." (1 Timothy 6:3-6)

2. *"Remind them of these things, and solemnly charge them in the presence of God not to wrangle about words, which is useless and leads to the ruin of the hearers. Be diligent to present yourself approved to God as a workman who does not need to be ashamed, accurately handling the word of truth."* (2 Timothy 2:14-16)

3. *"But refuse foolish and ignorant speculations, knowing that they produce quarrels. The Lord's bond-servant must not be quarrelsome, but be kind to all, able to teach, patient when wronged, with gentleness correcting those who are in opposition, if perhaps God may grant them repentance leading to the knowledge of the truth."* (2 Timothy 3:23-25)

C. Paul instructs pastors to address an issue from a <u>Biblical perspective</u> and not strive over the Word (2 Timothy 2:14-19).

D. If there is conflict having to do with a pastor or elder, the Word of God instructs us:

"Do not receive an accusation against an elder except on the basis of two or three witnesses. Those who continue in sin, rebuke in the presence of all, so that the rest also will be fearful of sinning." (1 Timothy 5:19-21)

E. The elders and deacons are responsible for members being accountable for loving one another (Philippians 1:1; 4:1).

F. Anytime a conflict is creating division in <u>the church, leaders</u> are commanded to address it (Titus 3:9-11), explained in chapter 1.

G. The church is not to allow believers to have unresolved conflicts:

1. Paul told the church of Philippi that they must resolve the conflict between Euodia and Syntyche in Philippians 4:2-3. Paul can state this in chapter 4 because he described for us how we should behave in chapters 1:27-20 and 2:1-5.

A Practical Application to Biblically Resolving Conflicts Among Leaders

A. When there was a serious conflict among the disciples concerning Paul going to the Gentiles or conflict between Paul and Barnabas concerning John called Mark, it was discussed and resolved among the leadership (Acts 15:1-12; 36-41).

B. If conflict concerning a doctrinal issue arises, it must be brought to the attention of the pastor. He serves as the primary teacher of the church (1 Timothy 4:11-16; 2 Timothy 4:1-5). It is then discussed, in a church with elders, among the elders. In a church where there are deacons, the pastor must seek out individuals in the deacon ministry who demonstrate what Acts 6:2-3 states — spiritual men who are wise to help research the issue Biblically (remember the Word of God provides us everything we need; 2 Timothy 3:17; 2 Peter 1:3-4). If the pastor is not comfortable with this group, he should try the Sunday School ministry or ministers in the church to see if there are others there who are spiritually mature and Biblically literate.

C. If an elder/deacon disagrees with a decision the pastor made in a meeting, they should meet with the pastor in a private meeting or address it during the elder/deacon meeting. He should not talk about it anywhere else even at home with his wife.

D. If members in the church body disagree with a decision the pastor made and come to the elder/deacon about it, the elder/deacon should:

1. First, send the member to talk with the pastor directly.

2. If the member begins talking with others in the church rather than the pastor, the elder/deacon should function based on chapter 1.

3. If the pastor is not present and the elder/deacon need to provide an answer to the member, the elder/deacon must work to

have a cohesive answer before responding (Numbers 11:16-30). They must then inform the pastor upon his return.

"But I say to you that everyone who is angry with his brother shall be guilty before the court; and whoever says to his brother, 'You good-for-nothing,' shall be guilty before the supreme court; and whoever says, 'You fool,' shall be guilty enough to go into the fiery hell. Therefore, if you are presenting your offering at the altar, and there remember that your brother has some-thing against you, leave your offering there before the altar and go; first be reconciled to your brother, and then come and present your offering. Make friends quickly with your opponent at law while you are with him on the way, so that your opponent may not hand you over to the judge, and the judge to the officer, and you be thrown into prison. Truly I say to you, you will not come out of there until you have paid up the last cent." (Matthew 5:22-26)

Preserving the Unity Within the Church:
Biblical principles for resolving conflicts in a Godly manner

1. Leaders based on the Word of God must be committed to loving one another (Romans 12:9-10; Matthew 22:37-40). Love = results from obeying God's Word because God is love (1 John 2:3-6, 9-11; 4:7-12,16). We cannot love without Him; that is why love highlights who is a disciple of Christ (John 13:34-35). Love is not based on someone's feelings or whether or not a leader agrees with an-other leader. Because God is love He shapes and directs how love is executed (1 John 4:7-11). Nowhere in scripture does God direct us to like anyone. He commands us to love them and He states that if we do not love, we do not have a truly intimate experience of who He is: *"Beloved, let us love one another, for love is from God; and everyone who loves is born of God and knows God. The one who does not love does not know God, for God is love."* (1 John 4:7-9) This pas-sage implies that the believer is not a spiritually maturing believer (1 John 2:3-6; John 13:34-35), they are in the flesh (Galatians 5:16-

21). When we read in verse 21 that a believer will "not inherit the kingdom of God," it means that this believer is not living under the direction of the Holy Spirit (Ephesians 1:13-14).

2. In the midst of an argument, we must *"never pay back evil for evil to anyone. Respect what is right in the sight of all men."* (Romans 12:17) When a man or woman thinks something is right, and it does not violate any scriptures, then that person's opinion needs to be respected (Romans 14). This means that they need to be heard, their comments valued. This is relative to each person which in turn creates healthy discussions and open dialogue. When believers are being led by the Spirit of God, therefore under the authority of the Word of God, the Holy Spirit directs them so that they have a cohesive movement forward. This is what we see take place in Acts 15.

3. Believers must pray for one another (James 5:16-17), and we must confess our sins to each other so that God heals us when necessary. It is required for those who are involved to live righteous lives. This removes gossip, self-righteousness, or a condemning spirit (Romans 8:1). This demonstration of humility allows each leader to remain spiritually focused which in turn leads to a Spirit-led body of believers functioning cohesively.

    For example, if a leader in the midst of a discussion becomes heated or says things that are offensive to another leader, the Spirit of God convicts them (John 16:8-11), and the Word of God directs them to go to their brother or sister (Matthew 5:21-26) and discuss what took place. Instead of the dispute dividing these leaders, it drives each person to submit to Christ under the direction of the Holy Spirit. This causes both persons to grow spiritually rather than quit the leadership group, leave the church, or walk around the church creating more strife by talking about the matter to others who are not a part of the group. This is what Paul tells Timothy, *"Remind them of these things, and solemnly charge them in the presence of God not to wrangle about words, which is useless and leads to the ruin of the hearers. Be diligent to present yourself approved to God as a workman who does not need to be ashamed, accurately handling the word of truth."* (2 Timothy 2:14-16; NASB)

4. Do not use unwholesome words when responding to one another (Ephesians 4:25-32), and allow bitterness, wrath, anger, clamor, or slander to develop. We are commanded to have our words be seasoned with salt (Colossians 4:6), and they cannot be filthy (Ephesians 5:3-4). They must be well thought out so that they build each person up (Ephesians 4:29). This is why a foundation of spiritually maturing leaders is everything.

   a. We are told not to even enter worship without resolving conflicts with other brothers and sisters in Christ (Matthew 5:21-24). In the case of a husband and wife, God will not even honor their worship (Malachi 3:13-16).

5. We must follow God's structure for loving our enemies (Matthew 5:43-48; Romans 12:19-21) no matter how emotionally charged we may become.

6. If one believer is angry with another, they must seek to obey James 1:19-21 and Ephesians 4:26. They must manage anger in the following manner (James 1:19-21):

   a. Be quick to hear.

   b. Slow to speak.

   c. Slow to anger.

   d. When anger is allowed to hang around in a relationship Satan gets a foothold (Ephesians 4:26-27). The Garden of Eden is a good reminder of what Satan can do to leaders and a marriage.

   e. It is important to obey the rules set by James because then we will function in the Spirit and not in the flesh. The flesh will lead to strife (Galatians 5:19-21).

7. When someone's sin is addressed, the focus must always be reconciliation:

a. It must be based on facts (Matthew 18:15-21).

b. It must be done in private and kept private (Matthew 18:15-21).

c. Must be done with a spirit of gentleness (Galatians 6:1).

d. To forgive one another (Matthew 6:14-15).

8. The church must challenge believers to grow spiritually because the fruit of spiritual growth erases persistent conflicts:

a. It does not allow arguments to persist (Ephesians 4:1-4; 5:1-2).

b. It allows people to find answers to every issue they may experience (2 Peter 1:3; Ephesians 5:15-18).

c. The fruit of spiritual growth leads to a lasting and loving relationship (Galatians 5:22-24) because it endures all things (long-suffering) and it is influenced by love, peace, and kindness.

d. It leads to unity that is sustained by the power of God (Ephesians 4:1-8; 5:21).

e. The lack of spiritual growth leads to a lot of trouble (Galatians 5:19-21). Carnality represents immaturity which leads to jealousy and strife (1 Corinthians 3:1-4). Leaders become angry when other leaders are promoted. They must win arguments, can go about not speaking to one another, form clicks within the group that gather together after church or sit together in church, and can even become confrontational when they do not get their way. This vividly took place with Christ and the Jewish leaders. It became so vicious they orchestrated Him being nailed to the cross. They took Christ before a secular court like you see some leaders do today to determine what happens to Him. They had great positions in the Mosaic system, but they were not spiritually led.

Conclusion

"Therefore if there is any encouragement in Christ, if there is any consolation of love, if there is any fellowship of the Spirit, if any affection and compassion, make my joy complete by being of the same mind, maintaining the same love, united in spirit, intent on one purpose. Do nothing from selfishness or empty conceit, but with humility of mind regard one another as more important than yourselves; do not merely look out for your own personal interests, but also for the interests of others. Have this attitude in yourselves which was also in Christ Jesus." (Philippians 2:1-3; Colossians 3:12-17)

"But we request of you, brethren, that you appreciate those who diligently labor among you, and have charge over you in the Lord and give you instruction, and that you esteem them very highly in love because of their work. Live in peace with one another. We urge you, brethren, admonish the unruly, encourage the fainthearted, help the weak, be patient with everyone. See that no one repays another with evil for evil, but always seek after that which is good for one another and for all people. Rejoice always; pray without ceasing; in everything give thanks; for this is God's will for you in Christ Jesus. Do not quench the Spirit; do not despise prophetic utterances. But examine everything carefully; hold fast to that which is good; abstain from every form of evil." (1 Thessalonians 5:12-22)

CHAPTER 3

Critiquing Each Other While Growing Together

How Are We Allowed to Critique a Fellow Christian?

"For if anyone thinks he is something when he is nothing, he deceives himself. But each one must examine his own work, and then he will have reason for boasting in regard to himself alone, and not in regard to another. For each one will bear his own load." (Galatians 6:3-5)

A. When we confront other believers, it must be for the purpose of their edification (Ephesians 4:29-32). These characteristics should never be a part of the process:

1. <u>Unwholesome words</u> – Corrupt, unfit, bad (speaking of a decaying fish or decaying tree) (Ephesians 5:4).

2. <u>Bitterness</u> – Spite that harbors resentment, keeps a score of wrongdoings, is ready to fly off the handle with their sharp biting tongue.

3. <u>Anger</u> – Flare of heated passion or frustration, a strong feeling that has a strong outburst (Matthew 5:21-22).

4. Wrath – Settled anger when the heart becomes a roaring furnace.

5. Clamor – Violent outbursts of a person who has completely lost their temper; yelling, one step from physical violence.

6. Slander – Abusive speech directed at others or even God. Root is blasphemy.

7. Malice – Mischief, the evil inclination of the mind, the perversity or baseness that takes delight in hurting or injuring others.

B. We must speak the truth with love (Ephesians 4:25) – the truth sets us free from manmade laws (Pharisaic laws – Colossians 2:6-8; Matthew 15:1-4; Mark 7:5-8), and from sin that can easily entangle us (Hebrews 12:1). *"It was for freedom that Christ set us free; therefore keep standing firm and do not be subject again to a yoke of slavery."* (Galatians 5:1)

1. Truth — We must make sure what we are talking about is truth (Matthew 18:16) – *"every word may be established."*

   a. It must not be an evaluation of their motives (based on what we think a person thinks or feels or intended). It must always be about obedience or lack of obedience to God's Word (Matthew 18:15-20; Galatians 6:1-5).

   b. We must not become involved in ignorant disputes based on speculations. This could cause a person to be captivated by demons (2 Timothy 2:23-26) and ruin those who hear (2 Timothy 2:14).

   c. We are commanded to turn believers back to the truth because this stimulates their maturing process (James 5:19-20).

2. Love — It must be done with gentleness, not self-serving, not rude or arrogant: (1 Corinthians 13:4-7).

   a. Love is defined by God, not our feelings our opinions (1 John 4:7-11; keyword is 'know,' verse 8). It is impossible to display His love when we do not know Him (1 John 2:3-6; meaning having a daily experience of the Spirit of God working in our lives).

The Spirit of God dwells in us (Ephesians 3:16) because He has been poured into us at the point of salvation (Titus 3:4-7) to work in us in the following manner (a summary):

- He is committed to us at the point of salvation forever (John 14:16-17).

- He convicts us of sin (John 16:7-11).

- He reminds us of God's Word (John 14:26).

- He illuminates the Word of God for us to understand (1 Corinthians 2:10-15).

- He comforts us in times of grief (John 14:6).

- He prays for us when we are in pain and don't know how to pray (Romans 8:26).

- He provides spiritual fruit that shapes our character when we choose to walk under the influence of the Spirit (Galatians 5:16-25).

- He guides us into a true understanding of God's Word (John 16:13) so that we can live free from the influences of the flesh (John 8:31-32).

b. When love led by the Holy Spirit comes out of us, then we will NOT demonstrate these characteristics:

- Arrogance — It does not come over as if the other person who is making the criticism is better (1 Corinthians 10:12; Galatians 6:3).

- Self-serving — We must not look out for our own personal interest (Philippians 2:1-5).

- Condemnation — It should be done with <u>kindness, mercy</u> (Colossians 3:12).

- It must be done with a <u>readiness to forgive</u> — longsuffering (Colossians 3:12-13).

- Complaints — We are not allowed to complain <u>against one another</u> (Colossians 3:13; Philippians 2:14-15).

- Grumblings — We are not allowed to murmur or grumble <u>against one another</u> (James 5:9).

C. 1 Thessalonians 5:14 instructs us to confront the unruly.

   1. This relates to those believers who do not obey God as it relates to how they treat other believers, function within the church, and how they respect their pastor (1 Timothy 3:14-15; Titus 2:15; Hebrews 13:17).

   2. These believers' function in a disorderly manner (1 Corinthians 14:40). There is no respect given for the organizational structure of the church (1 Timothy 3:15). In 1 Thessalonians 5:12-14, it seems to relate to how they responded to those in leadership (there were no elders and deacons, as yet, but there were those who diligently served in those capacities in helping the church) and were not committed to *"live in peace with one another"* (vs. 13).

D. Grace should abound in the following manner:

   1. We must speak the truth in love (Ephesians 4:25).

   2. Forgive one another (Matthew 6:13; Colossians 3:12-13).

   3. Be patient when wronged (2 Timothy 2:24). Longsuffering — seventy times seven (Matthew 18:21-22).

E. Steps that can keep us all when emotions may be strong:

   1. Focus only on the facts.

2. Evaluate the facts based on the Word of God.

3. Work out how the issue can be resolved based on God's structure.

4. After the above is implemented, then feelings can be considered. When feelings are first, relationships can be destructive.

"Let love be without hypocrisy. Abhor what is evil; cling to what is good. Be devoted to one another in brotherly love; give preference to one another in honor; not lagging behind in diligence, fervent in spirit, serving the Lord; rejoicing in hope, persevering in tribulation, devoted to prayer, contributing to the needs of the saints, practicing hospitality." (Romans 12:9-13)

What Are We Not Allowed to Do?

"But you, why do you judge your brother? Or you again, why do you regard your brother with contempt? For we will all stand before the judgment seat of God. For it is written, "AS I LIVE, SAYS THE LORD, EVERY KNEE SHALL BOW TO ME, AND EVERY TONGUE SHALL GIVE PRAISE TO GOD." So then each one of us will give an account of himself to God." (Romans 14:10-12)

A. A believer's behavior cannot be evaluated when the person doing the evaluation struggles with the same sin (Matthew 7:1-5; Romans 2:1-3).

B. It must not be based on a legalistic process (Matthew 15:1-9; 23:13-36). We cannot judge another by manmade rules we create (Colossians 2:8). Some examples are:

1. Some people believe that women should never wear pants (Deuteronomy 22:5 – the issue is cross-dressing).

2. Some people believe that a woman's dress should be to her an-

kle. The issue is modesty so that a woman focuses more on her character development than just on how she looks (1 Peter 3:2-5).

3. Some people believe that women should only have certain hairstyles.

4. The church must sing from hymnals. It must be all hymns when the scripture teaches hymns, 'spiritual songs, and singing with thanksgiving in our hearts' — praise songs (Colossians 3:16).

5. Deacons must wear gloves when they do the Lord's Supper.

"Whatever you do in word or deed, do all in the name of the Lord Jesus, giving thanks through Him to God the Father." (Colossians 3:17)

C. We must not criticize someone in anger (Ephesians 4:26).

D. We cannot have endless arguments over issues (James 2:14; 4:1-4).

E. If someone offends us, we must go to them focused on restoration, not isolation and degradation (Matthew 5:22-26; 18:15-20).

1. An offense is not when someone does something we don't like. The word means to violate a law or ruling. The offense takes place when the person violates the Word of God as it relates to us. To love God is to keep His commandments which leads to us loving our neighbor (Matthew 22:36-40). So we do not love our neighbor when we violate the Word of God.

F. We are not allowed to take each other to court (1 Corinthians 6:1-8).

"Therefore, confess your sins to one another, and pray for one another so that you may be healed. The effective prayer of a righteous man can accomplish much." (James 5:16)

How to Receive Criticism from a Fellow Christian

"For we are not bold to class or compare ourselves with some of those who commend themselves; but when they measure themselves by themselves and compare themselves with themselves, they are without understanding. But we will not boast beyond our measure, but within the measure of the sphere which God apportioned to us as a measure, to reach even as far as you." (2 Corinthians 10:12-14)

A. Once the above process is properly applied the following should occur:

1. We must accept it for our edification (Ephesians 4:29).

2. We must accept it as part of the equipping process that leads to knowledge and unity (Ephesians 4:14-16). There is a gift of knowledge, wisdom, and discernment which can be helpful when used under the authority of scripture guided by the Holy Spirit (1 Peter 4:10).

3. We must display love and not harbor resentment towards a person (James 3:14).

B. If another believer does hurtful things we must not pay back evil for evil (Romans 12:17; 1 Thessalonians 5:15):

1. We must not curse (Romans 12:14; Ephesians 5:3-4).

2. If we get angry, we must not sin (Ephesians 4:26).

3. Seek to make friends with those who seek to be enemies as much as it depends on the person being criticized (Matthew 5:25; Romans 12:14-21). God does not say we have to resolve this (Jesus, while on earth, did not resolve His disagreements with Jewish leaders). God expects us to keep His Word as we relate even to those who choose to be enemies. Remember love is not a feeling. Love is directed and guided by the implementation of God's Word through the ministry of the Holy Spirit.

C. If what we are doing is a stumbling block to another believer, we must adjust so that they can continue with their growth process (1 Corinthians 8:7-13).

D. We must respond in love (John 14:34-35; Romans 12:10).

E. *"Therefore if you are presenting your offering at the altar, and there remember that your brother has something against you, leave your offering there before the altar and go; first be reconciled to your brother, and then come and present your offering."* (Matthew 5:23-25)

F. 12 Rules for Successful Conflict Resolution

1. Examine yourself — admit your own faults.

2. Limit conflict to present — "DON'T USE YESTERDAY'S PROBLEMS FOR TODAY'S AMMUNITION."

3. Keep to one issue.

4. Use "I" messages.

5. Don't use character generalizations.

6. Don't counterattack.

7. Don't mind read.

8. Deal with conflicts promptly.

9. Control your emotions.

10. Don't keep track of wins or losses. Remember, if one person wins in an argument, both people lose.

11. Set foul limits.

12. Makes some rules.

A special word from Dr. Cannings:

"TIME SPENT FIGHTING IS TIME WASTED. ONCE SPENT, IT BRINGS NOTHING BUT MEMORIES."

Conclusion

There are many key points to be learned and applied when we critique our brethren, but the root of our words and actions must be done in love.

"My brethren, if any among you strays from the truth and one turns him back, let him know that he who turns a sinner from the error of his way will save his soul from death and will cover a multitude of sins." (James 5:19-20)

"So, as those who have been chosen of God, holy and beloved, put on a heart of compassion, kindness, humility, gentleness and patience; bearing with one another, and forgiving each other, whoever has a complaint against anyone; just as the Lord forgave you, so also should you. Beyond all these things put on love, which is the perfect bond of unity. Let the peace of Christ rule in your hearts, to which indeed you were called in one body; and be thankful." (Colossians 3:12-15)

"For he who in this way serves Christ is acceptable to God and approved by men. So then we pursue the things which make for peace and the building up of one another." (Romans 14:18-19)

CHAPTER 4

Resolving Difficulties While Getting the Job Done

Introduction

Difficulties and conflicts can stagnant ministries, divide them, or even destroy them. There is not a leader in the Bible who did not encounter difficulties or conflicts. Abraham in reference to Lot, the situation with Hagar, David and Saul, Job being tried by God, Nehemiah rebuilding the walls and all the people who opposed him, and the list goes on. What is amazing is that despite everything these individuals and others completed what God placed before them to accomplish. Paul says it this way, "*For I am already being poured out as a drink offering, and the time of my departure has come. I have fought the good fight, I have finished the course, I have kept the faith; in the future there is laid up for me the crown of righteousness, which the Lord, the righteous Judge, will award to me on that day; and not only to me, but also to all who have loved His appearing.*" (2 Timothy 4:6-8)

We approach ministry expecting everything to go well because it is the Lord's church. When things do work out, we become more committed to winning the battle than completing the task God has provided to us. This chapter is focused on how we can remain focused despite the struggles we can experience in ministry.

Resolving Conflicts or Difficulties — Summary Review

Summary from the first two chapters

> *"We urge you, brethren, admonish the unruly, encourage the faint-hearted, help the weak, be patient with everyone. See that no one repays another with evil for evil, but always seek after that which is good for one another and for all people. Rejoice always; pray without ceasing; in everything give thanks; for this is God's will for you in Christ Jesus. Do not quench the Spirit."* (1 Thessalonians 5:14-19)

Leaders' Responsibilities

1. Paul instructed pastors to function in this manner:

    a. *"If anyone advocates a different doctrine and does <u>not agree with sound words</u>, those of our Lord Jesus Christ, and with the doctrine conforming to godliness, <u>he is conceited and understands nothing</u>; but he has a morbid interest in controversial questions and disputes about words, out of which arise envy, strife, abusive language, evil suspicions, and constant friction between men of depraved mind and deprived of the truth, who suppose that godliness is a means of gain. But godliness actually is a means of great gain when accompanied by contentment."* (1 Timothy 6:3-6)

    b. *"Remind them of these things, and solemnly charge them <u>in the presence of God not to wrangle about words</u>, which is useless and leads <u>to the ruin of the hearers</u>. Be diligent to present yourself approved to God as a workman who does not need to be ashamed, accurately handling the word of truth."* (2 Timothy 2:14-16)

    c. *"<u>But refuse foolish and ignorant speculations, knowing that they produce quarrels. The Lord's bond-servant must not be quarrelsome</u>, but be kind to all, able to teach, patient when wronged, with gentleness correcting those who are in opposition, if perhaps God may grant them repentance leading to the knowledge of the truth."* (2 Timothy 2:23-25)

- Paul instructs pastors to address issues from a Biblical perspective while striving over the Word (2 Timothy 2:14-19).

- Leaders must come alongside the pastor to assist him in providing leadership in critical times (Numbers 11:16-18):

  » God spoke to only Moses throughout this passage.

  » Moses spirit was transferred to the leaders — unity is strength.

- **If there is conflict having to do with a pastor or an elder, the Word of God instructs us:**

  » *"Do not receive an accusation against an elder <u>except on the basis of two or three witnesses</u>. Those who continue in sin, rebuke in the presence of all, so that the rest also will be fearful of sinning."* (1 Timothy 5:19-21)

2. The elders and deacons are responsible for not allowing believers to continuously have conflicts that go unaddressed (Philippians 1:1; 4:1).

   a. Paul told the church of Philippi that they must resolve the conflict between Euodia and Syntyche in Philippians 4:2-3. Paul gives this directive because he has already described how we should behave in chapters 1:27-20 and 2:1-5.

   b. Holding leaders and members accountable to this process can lead to spiritual growth (Romans 12:9-10; Matthew 22:37-40; 1 John 4:7-11).

   c. Holding members accountable to this process can also lead to spirit-filled worship experiences (Matthew 5:21-24).

      - **Anytime a conflict is creating division, the pastor is commanded to address it (Titus 3:9-11).**

      - **As with pastors, whenever members see conflicts creating division in the church, they are commanded to address it**

(Romans 16:17-20; 1 Thessalonians 5:14; 2 Thessalonians 3:10-11).

The Mindset that Leads to Resolving Difficulties

1. Do not run from them as Elijah did (1 Kings 18:4,13-46 — see how it empowered Ahab even more). When he focused on the power of God and worked through difficult situations, like the prophets of Baal, he delivered a nation from sin, refocused them to God, and grew in favor with the people. Christ warns the disciples to function in the same manner (Matthew 10:26-39). Christ's point was, *"Do not think that I came to bring peace on the earth: I did not come to bring peace, but a sword."* (Matthew 10:34).

2. To not stand up the principles of God in the midst of conflict is to decide to be a follower (Peter and his denial of Christ – Matthew 26:69-75. Peter was warned in Luke 5:11).

3. Nehemiah stood alone when he prayed and went before the king (Nehemiah 1). He stood alone when he went before the people (Nehemiah 2:20-24) and he stood alone when the enemies of the Israelites decided to attack him (Nehemiah 6:1-14).

4. When we seek to save our lives for our sakes, Christ states that is when we lose it. *"And Jesus answered them, saying, 'The hour has come for the Son of Man to be glorified. Truly, truly, I say to you, unless a grain of wheat falls into the earth and dies, it remains alone; but if it dies, it bears much fruit. He who loves his life loses it, and he who hates his life in this world will keep it to life eternal. If anyone serves Me, he must follow Me; and where I am, there My servant will be also; if anyone serves Me, the Father will honor him."* (John 12:23-25)

    a. Go; behold, I send you out as lambs in the midst of wolves. (Luke 10:3-4)

5. Paul told Timothy to maintain this mindset because Timothy was discouraged and afraid (2 Timothy 1:3-7). *"Now you followed my*

teaching, conduct, purpose, faith, patience, love, perseverance, persecutions, and sufferings, such as happened to me at Antioch, at Iconium and at Lystra; what persecutions I endured, and out of them all the Lord rescued me! Indeed, all who desire to live godly in Christ Jesus will be persecuted. But evil men and impostors will proceed from bad to worse, deceiving and being deceived." (2 Timothy 3:10-14)

Resolving Conflicts is Critical to Spiritual Well-Being of the Church

1. Members can become dull of hearing because they no longer desire the truth (Matthew 13:15; 2 Timothy 4:3-5; Hebrews 5:11 – in this Hebrews passage, a willingness to grow spiritually would have created a teachable spirit – Hebrews 4:12-14).

2. When leaders focus on more speculations rather than facts (the truth), demons can infiltrate the church creating division and anarchy (2 Timothy 3:23-26).

3. When trials and worries do not lead to experiencing spiritual growth like James 1:2-4 explains, it creates, *"The seed which fell among the thorns, these are the ones who have heard, and as they go on their way they are choked with worries and riches and pleasures of this life and bring no fruit to maturity."* (Luke 8:14)

4. When leaders are not growing spiritually [If all they seek is Bible knowledge but do not use the work to grow (Romans 12:2), they become arrogant and useless (1 Corinthians 8:1-3)]. They can become as wolves (Acts 20:28-31). Then the church ends up being attacked from the inside.

5. When the church is not dominated by the Word, nor is it structured according to His directive, it can execute ministry in truth. Then ministry can become religious, committed to its traditions rather than to Christ (Matthew 15:1-2, 7-9; Colossians 2:8).

    a. Remember that teaching false doctrine, no matter how simple the issue is, stirs demonic activity in the church (Matthew 24:11; 1 Timothy 4:1-2, 6-10).

b. Human wisdom is demonic (James 3:14-15). This is why the scriptures teach us not to lean to our own understanding (Proverbs 3:5-6).

Remove 'Holy Cows' for the Sake of Progress

Tradition by instruction, narrative, precept, etc. 2a objectively, that which is delivered, the substance of a teaching. 2b of the body of precepts, esp. ritual, which in the opinion of the later Jews were orally delivered by Moses and orally transmitted in unbroken succession to subsequent generations, which precepts, both illustrating and expanding the written law, as they did were to be obeyed with equal reverence.[1]

The Ills of Tradition (Matthew 15:1-3; Mark 7:6-9; Colossians 2:8)

1. It can lead to scripture being violated (Mark 7:6-9).

2. It causes believers to follow human philosophy (Colossians 2:8). It takes believers away from the doctrines they must become rooted in (Mark 7-9).

3. It causes believers to have crooked paths (Proverbs 3:5-6) because they then lean on their own man-made understanding.

4. It creates strongholds for the flesh (2 Corinthians 10:2-5) and for Satan (2 Timothy 2:23-26).

5. Man-made philosophy leads to dissension in the church (1 Timothy 6:3-4).

---

1 Strong, J. 1996. *The exhaustive concordance of the Bible: Showing every word of the test of the common English version of the canonical books, and every occurrence of each word in regular order.* (electronic ed.). Woodside Bible Fellowship.: Ontario

    a. The church becomes more of what every man believes it should be rather than what God says it must be (Judges 21:25).

6. Human traditions do not lead to godliness. God's traditions lead to fulfilling the purposes of the church (Matthew 28:19-20; Colossians 1:28-29).

Traditions Worth Following (2 Thessalonians 2:15; 1 Corinthians 11:1-2)

1. Traditions were those delivered by the apostles (1 Corinthians 11:1-2, 23; 15:1-2). Paul says that we must hold to these traditions (2 Thessalonians 2:15 – The word 'hold' is a present imperative which means he is commanding us to make this a habitual action):

    a. Preaching the gospel.

    b. Lord's Supper.

    c. Baptism.

    d. The sound teaching of doctrines (Acts 2:42).

    e. Giving (1 Corinthians 16:1-2).

    f. Church attendance (Hebrews 10:23-26).

    g. Worship (Acts 2:42-43; Colossians 3:15-17; Hebrews 23-26).

    h. Fellowship (Acts 2:42).

    i. Prayer (Acts 2:42).

    j. Leadership structure (1 Timothy 3:1-15).

    k. Church discipline (Matthew 18:15-20; Galatians 6:1-2).

"Now we command you, brethren, in the name of our Lord Jesus Christ, that you keep away from every brother who leads an unruly life and not according to the tradition which you received from us. For you yourselves know how you ought to follow our ex-

ample, because we did not act in an undisciplined manner among you..." (2 Thessalonians 3:6-7)

Getting the Job Done in the Midst of Difficulties

"Therefore, since we have so great a cloud of witnesses surrounding us, let us also lay aside every encumbrance and the sin which so easily entangles us, and let us run with endurance the race that is set before us, fixing our eyes on Jesus, the author and perfecter of faith, who for the joy set before Him endured the cross, despising the shame, and has sat down at the right hand of the throne of God. For consider Him who has endured such hostility by sinners against Himself, so that you will not grow weary and lose heart." (Hebrews 12:1-3)

Leading in Crisis Situations Means the Leader Must Take the First Step

"And without faith it is impossible to please Him for he who comes to God must believe that He is and that He is a rewarder of those who seek Him." (Hebrews 11:6)

1. There are some great examples in scripture that made a profound difference in the development of the church across the world:

   a. When Barnabas saw the zeal of the brethren at Antioch he went and got Paul, then known as Saul (Acts 11:19-26). This made a tremendous difference and helped Paul move from Tarsus to the mission field God called him to. This took place before the Jerusalem council meeting (Acts 15).

   b. *"I am writing these things to you, hoping to come to you before long; but in case I am delayed, I write so that you will know how one ought to conduct himself in the household of God, which is the church of the living God, the pillar and support of the truth."* (1 Timothy 3:14-15)

c. Daniel took initiative, as a result of His Biblical convictions, and became the wisest man among wise men (Daniel 1:8-13). Daniel ended up setting things in order for his three friends.

d. There are several steps that Daniel took when he took the initiative to deal with a difficult situation:

- He believed God for His Word (1:8-9).

- He did not succumb to the pressure of his peers (1:13).

- He trusted God to provide the results (1:12). The results God provides can cause unbelievers to believe (1:14-16).

- He chose not to be afraid of man (Joshua 1:8-9; 2 Tim. 1:7), but rather to fear God (Psalm 128:1-2). Fear and faith do not mix; think of it as oil and water.

- He was persistent about his commitment (1:9-11).

- Daniel lived a life of integrity (Ezekiel 14:14; 14:20; 28:3).

e. Elijah took the initiative and made a major difference in preventing the false worship from spreading (1 Kings 18:20-35).

2. The heart of a committed servant (servant leadership will be discussed in a later chapter) always makes a way out of no way. This is because a servant only needs to see a need in order to be stimulated to take the initiative to serve.

a. David stood before Goliath rather than run and began his career as Israel's greatest leader. This mindset was the nature of David's development as a leader (1 Samuel 17:31-58).

b. Nehemiah, a cupbearer, made up in his heart to serve God and he made a major difference (Nehemiah 2:17-20).

c. The disciples needed help providing services to the widows, as described in Acts 6:1-6, and thus the office of deacons was born.

d. Dorcas realized the need of the widows and faithfully served them, creating a great testimony for the glory of God (Acts 9:32-43).

e. A leader exercises initiative by being willing to serve without anyone requesting their service. They see a need and they respond (John 13:1-17), as shown by Jesus washing the disciples' feet; Acts 28:2-3, and Paul gathering wood for everyone who survived the shipwreck.

3. Paul's ministry was full of zeal (Philippians 3:7-16; 2 Timothy 4:6-8). He said that even though he is the least of the apostles, he works harder than all of them (1 Corinthians 15:10).

a. Are they servants of Christ? — I speak as if insane — I more so; in far more labors, in far more imprisonments, beaten times without number, often in danger of death. (2 Corinthians 11:23).

The Attitude a Leader Must Have to Get the Job Done

"The Lord's lovingkindnesses indeed never cease, for His compassions never fail. They are new every morning; great is Your faithfulness. "The Lord is my portion," says my soul, "Therefore I have hope in Him." The Lord is good to those who wait for Him, to the person who seeks Him. It is good that he waits silently for the salvation of the Lord." (Lamentations 3:22-26)

1. Pray for God's power (Nehemiah 1:5-6).

2. The church must be committed to discipling leaders (2 Timothy 2:2; Hebrews 13:7-8) and members (Ephesians 4:12-13; Colossians 1:28-29).

3. Leaders must view the Word of God as sufficient for everything the church has to do (2 Peter 1:3-4; 2 Timothy 3:16-17).

a. Keep the church pure and driven by the truth (1 Timothy 3:15) so that church represents Christ powerfully (Ephesians 3:10).

4. Leaders must view themselves as always needing God to empower them to serve Him (2 Corinthians 3:3-5).

5. Leaders must focus more on completing task, not competing with each other (2 Corinthians 10:12-13; Philippians 1:14-18).

6. No matter the difficulties, leaders must remain faithful to God's Word, their families, and the church's vision, and must respect the leadership structure of the church (1 Timothy 3:15; 1 Corinthians 15:58).

7. Leaders must always strive to maintain unity (John 17:23; Philippians 2:1-6).

Getting the Job Done

1. A leader must always bear in mind the following things:

   a. The church's vision.

   b. The church's Doctrinal Statement.

   c. The philosophy statement for that ministry area.

   d. The goals and objectives for that ministry.

   e. Each leader's ministry description (job description). This causes everyone to remain in their lane, complementing each other for a great team effort.

2. The leader must serve the people (Mark 10:42-44) leading them to their ministry goals and objectives.

   a. Must seek out their ideas and try to incorporate them. This makes team members feel valued and creates more energy for long-lasting participation.

   b. Remember that they are individuals who may have their own problems. Seek to serve them. Keep with their personal pains and struggles because this is the greatest moments of spiritual growth (James 1:2-4).

c. Delegate clearly outlined responsibilities so that they feel a sense of responsibility as a part of the team (discussed in a later chapter).

d. Set a time table of expectations.

e. Never forget our spiritual responsibility to disciple each person.

f. Provide them room to fail.

Jay Adams says the following, "I am responsible for two categories of work: the kind I like to do and the kind I have to do."

3. A leader must know what it takes to make that particular ministry work. Then the leader must pray continuously (1 Thessalonians 5:17), and actively seek out those individuals who have the following criteria:

a. A heart for that particular area.

b. A teachable spirit (2 Timothy 2:2).

c. A willingness to serve others (Mark 10:41-44).

d. A strong commitment to a specific area in that particular ministry, e.g., spiritual gift (1 Peter 4:10).

e. A demonstrated respect for the leadership structure by the manner in which they handle their disagreements (Hebrews 13:17).

4. A leader must always bear in mind that if they are in God's will, God will send workers for His harvesting.

"So, the lesson in all this is faith. Trust the Lord. He has promised to supply and He will. But as in every other aspect of life, you must exercise faith. Believe God. And trust Him to provide the right kind of help." (Jay Adams. "Be the Leader God Meant You to Be." Page 84)

5. The leader must "Focus on Objectives, Not Obstacles:"

"Negative attitudes can carry over in our outlook toward a task we're involved in. It can make us problem-centered rather than goal-centered." (Jay Adams. "Be the Leader God Meant You to Be." Page 85)

a. This does not mean that a leader will ignore obstacles. It just means that they must have the mind of an overcomer (Philippians 4:13).

b. When we view the hall of faith in Hebrews 11, we see many of God's people who are credited for their faith. Not just because they believed in God, but also because they plowed their way through obstacles by trusting, depending, and following God's direction.

- Faith in God is the key to all of this. Always bearing in mind that this is God's way of working through each leader not each leader's way of working through God. To stop when there are obstacles is to prevent God from working through us.

- Hebrews 11:1 says, *"Now faith is the assurance of things hoped for, the conviction of things not seen."*

Conclusion

A leader must believe they can do the impossible (Matthew 17:20; 19:26) because they believe that God is able to do the impossible through them. These leaders do not view problems as things that stop them but instead, they are as obstacles that grow them. *"And not only this, but we also exult in our tribulation knowing that tribulations brings about perseverance; and perseverance, proven character; and proven character, hope; and hope does not disappoint, because the love of God has been poured out within our hearts through the Holy Spirit who was given to us."* (Romans 5:3-5) The leader becomes so absorbed in God's purposes that the obstacles placed before them become greater experiences of God. *"What then shall we say to these things? If God is for us, who is against us?"* (Romans 8:31)

Many churches experience mediocrity today because leaders are unwilling to test God at His Word for a greater experience of His might and power. Churches become limited by man's ability, or lack of ability, to complete a task, rather than God's promises that makes all things possible (Romans 4:18-21).

1 Corinthians 15:58 — *"Therefore, my beloved brethren, be steadfast, immovable, always abounding in the work of the Lord, knowing that your toil is not in vain in the Lord."*

CHAPTER 5

Identifying Christian Leaders for the 21ˢᵗ Century Church

Introduction

The main focus for seeking out potential leaders is to ensure that once they are selected, they remain teachable and they retain a servant's heart. Through this right attitude, the discipleship and testing process is effective for the spiritual development of the church. In the following passage, notice that the spiritual development of a congregation will not take place if leaders are not striving based on the power of the Holy Spirit working within them. *"We proclaim Him, admonishing every man and teaching every man with all wisdom, so that we may present every man complete in Christ. For **this purpose,** also I labor, striving according to His power, which mightily works within me."* (Colossians 1:28-29)

What makes a leader great is how they transition from the flesh to the Spirit (Mark 10:41-44; John 21:15-17). This is also crucial because, in the difficult times, the leader can effectively resist the attacks of Satan; *"You are from God, little children, and have overcome them; because greater is He who is in you than He who is in the world."* (1 John 4:4)

When leaders are not growing spiritually, they can become more caught up in their titles than in their ministry function (Matthew 23:13-36). They are more focused on the esteem the church provides than in caring for God's flock (Mark 10:35-40). They can become leaders who are not teachable, which is the key to what Paul instructs Timothy to focus on. *"The things which you have heard from me in the presence of many witnesses, entrust these to faithful men who will be able to teach others also."* (2 Timothy 2:2) Please note that not until the disciples became true followers of Christ (Christ had to spend forty more days after His death to ensure they surrender to Him), did He tell them to go make disciples (Matthew 28:19-20). Until Peter committed to love Christ with all his heart, soul, and mind, Christ did not instruct Peter to feed His lambs (John 21:15-17).

A Guideline for Identifying Potential Leaders

A Spiritual Organism (the church is the body of Christ) Requires Spiritually Minded Leaders

1. Believers that actively demonstrate a commitment to discipleship (Luke 14:24-27; John 15:1-8). These are believers who, on their own initiative, are committed to studying and applying God's Word to their mind and heart (Hebrews 13:7-8). These believers are recognized by their willingness to be in the growing experiences of the church, to faithfully serve, and to be accountable to others (James 5:16-18). These potential leaders change lives by their example. This is the focus on discipleship:

    a. "... teaching them to observe...." (Matthew 28:20).

    b. "...imitate their faith..." (Hebrews 13:8).

2. If married, a leader must demonstrate a commitment to their family (Ephesians 5:32; 1 Timothy 3:4). This is seen when their spouse and children demonstrate a sincere respect for them.

    a. When a leader, if a man, does not manage his family well (1 Timothy 3:1-13) or live with his wife in an understanding way, his prayers are not answered (1 Peter 3:7).

    b. If the leader is a woman and she is not hospitable and/or is not committed to preserving what she and her husband established for their home, she will not be effective as a leader (1 Timothy 5:9-10).

c. If single, his or her life must demonstrate a devotion to Christ (1 Corinthians 7:32-35), as in the case of Dorcas (Acts 9:32-43).

3. Must not be a recent convert (1 Timothy 3:6).

4. Needs to be someone who loves other believers (John 13:34-35; Philippians 2:1-5). A commitment to love, even those who may be enemies, demonstrates a sincere commitment to Christ (Romans 12:9-21).

5. Needs to be someone who is trustworthy and reliable (2 Timothy 2:2).

6. Needs to be someone who is teachable (2 Timothy 2:2, 15).

7. If they are being trained to be a deacon, they must demonstrate a commitment to holiness and have the gift of service (Acts 6:3). If this person is not serving faithfully and, of their own initiative, engage to volunteer for the most menial task, they probably do not have the gift of service.

8. Leaders must recognize their insufficiency (2 Corinthians 3:5), and their need for the work of the Holy Spirit through Christ, before they can ever be totally effective (Moses in Exodus 3:11-12, Numbers 11:16-17; Gideon in Judges 6:15; Jeremiah in Jeremiah 1:6; Paul in 2 Corinthians 12:9-10, 2 Timothy 3:17).

a. When a leader approaches leadership as if they 'got it' and just need to move to ordination they most times become the most difficult people to lead. This is because they lean towards depending on their own abilities and talents.

Leaders Must Demonstrate an Attitude That Leads to Effective Ministry

1. I am purposefully repeating that leaders must faithfully serve in a ministry prior to being looked at for a leadership position (Acts 16:1-3; Ephesians 4:12).

2. Christian leaders <u>are servants</u>: (Matthew 20:27, 28; Mark 10:41-45; Philippians 2:5-7). *"Leaders in the church exist to facilitate the ministry of the whole body; they are not appointed to dominate or control the body."* (James E. Means, page 47)

3. They must not be argumentative (1 Timothy 6:3-5; 2 Timothy 2:14, 24; Proverbs 17:19).

4. A believer who consistently demonstrates support of the church's leadership structure (Hebrews 13:17; Matthew 16:21-23; Luke 5:1-11).

5. Must be more committed to the Word of God than traditions; 'holy cows' (Colossians 2:6-8; Matthew 15:2-9).

6. A believer who is a faithful giver and has demonstrated this for some time (Luke 12:31-34).

7. A believer who faithfully attends worship, Bible study, special church meetings (Hebrews 10:23-25), and leads their family to do the same.

8. A leader that will be effective must be flexible (1 Corinthians 16:6-7; 2 Corinthians 1:15-17; Acts 16:6).

9. An effective leader is someone who will be thorough (Matthew 28:19-20; Colossians 1:27-28; John 17:4,8.).

10. An effective leader is someone who does not run from challenges (1 Corinthians 16:9; 2 Corinthians 4:10).

11. Leaders must work for oneness (John 17:20-23) and takes action against those who create division (Romans 16:17-18; 2 Thessalonians 3:14-15; Titus 3:9-11).

Conclusion

Let us all be committed to building up the kingdom of God in and through the church (Ephesians 1:22-23).

This will allow the power, authority, and work of Christ, through the Holy Spirit, to be manifested to everyone. This process blesses the church, our families, and us. We must trust Him and allow Him to be head of the church (Colossians 1:17-20) so that we can, through Him, impact lives in the church, the community, and the world.

CHAPTER 6

Servant Leadership

Introduction

Many people serve today because of the expectations placed upon them. Some serve because they do not want to disappoint the pastor, while others hold positions because they were assigned to it and it provides them respect among the congregants, family, and the community. Even though these individuals may accomplish many tasks like it was with the leadership Christ encountered, their leadership does not stimulate spiritual growth among those they serve. Leaders should be life changers because Christ instructed leaders to make disciples. This is the ultimate purpose (Matthew 28:19) of the equipping of the saints for the work of service, to the building up of the body of Christ; *"… until we all attain to the unity of the faith, and of the knowledge of the Son of God, to a mature man, to the measure of the stature which belongs to the fullness of Christ. … from whom the whole body, being fitted and held together by what every joint supplies, according to the proper working of each individual part, causes the growth of the body for the building up of itself in love."* (Ephesians 4:12-13,16)

Life-Changing Leadership Serves from the Heart

A. A leader that serves because they sincerely love God and His people truly makes a difference:

1. Paul's concern for people is vividly portrayed in 1 Thessalonians 2:7: *"But we proved to be gentle among you, as a nursing mother tenderly cares for her own children. Having so fond an affection for you, we were well-pleased to impart to you not only the gospel of God but also our own lives, because you had become very dear to us."*

2. A lack of love exposes the level of one's spiritual growth (1 John 2:9-11; 4:12-14, 20).

3. *"We give thanks to God always for all of you, making mention of you in our prayers; <u>constantly bearing in mind your work of faith and labor of love</u> and steadfastness of hope in our Lord Jesus Christ in the presence of our God and Father, knowing, brethren beloved by God, His choice of you."* (1 Thessalonians 1:2-5)

B. Christ showed more interest in <u>the heart of a servant</u> before He instructed the servant to serve (John 21:15-17). Three times Christ asked, *"Peter, do you love me...."* Loving Christ was most important because, *"Teacher, which is the great commandment in the Law?" And He said to him, 'YOU SHALL LOVE THE LORD YOUR GOD WITH ALL YOUR HEART, AND WITH ALL YOUR SOUL, AND WITH ALL YOUR MIND.' This is the great and foremost commandment. The second is similar, 'YOU SHALL LOVE YOUR NEIGHBOR AS YOURSELF.' On these two commandments depend the whole Law and the Prophets."* (Matthew 22:36-40)

C. The heart of a <u>committed servant</u> always makes a way out of no way. This is because a servant only needs to see a need in order to be stimulated to take the initiative to serve.

1. <u>Nehemiah, a cup bearer, made up in his heart</u> to serve God and he made a major difference (Nehemiah 2:17-20).

2. <u>Needing help servicing widows</u> in Acts 6, the disciples directed the people to choose <u>godly men who were servants</u> (vs. 1-6).

3. Jesus washed the disciples' feet when no servant was available (John 13:5-10).

4. Paul saw the need to gather wood after being shipwrecked (Acts 28:2-3).

5. There are many examples of how committed servants make profound impacts for God's glory. Here are a few:

   a. *"Thus, Hezekiah did throughout all Judah; and he did what was good, right and true before the LORD his God. <u>Every work which he began in the service of the house of God in law and in commandment, seeking his God, he did with all his heart and prospered.</u>"* (2 Chronicles 31:20-21)

   b. *"<u>Whatever your hand finds to do, do it with all your might</u>; for there is no activity or planning or knowledge or wisdom in Sheol where you are going."* (Ecclesiastes 9:10)

   c. *"When I heard these words, I sat down and wept and mourned for days; and I was fasting and praying before the God of heaven. I said, "I beseech You, O LORD God of heaven, the great and awesome God, who preserves the covenant and lovingkindness for those who love Him and keep His commandments, let Your ear now be attentive and Your eyes open to hear the prayer of Your servant which I am praying before You now, day and night, on behalf of the sons of Israel Your servants, confessing the sins of the sons of Israel which we have sinned against You; I and my father's house have sinned."* (Nehemiah 1:4-7)

   d. *"<u>I press on toward the goal for the prize</u> of the upward call of God in Christ Jesus. Let us, therefore, as many as are perfect, have this attitude; and if in anything you have a different attitude, God will reveal that also to you; however, let us keep living by that same standard to which we have attained."* (Philippians 3:14-16)

   e. *"<u>Whatever you do, do your work heartily, as for the Lord rather than for men</u>, knowing that from the Lord you will receive the reward of the inheritance. It is the Lord Christ whom you serve. For he who does wrong will receive the consequences of*

the wrong which he has done, and that without partiality."
(Colossians 3:23-25)

"Whole-heartedness and zeal are the outgrowths of a love that burns in the leader's heart. From there it spreads to the hearts and lives of others, who catch the flame of that spirit." (Jay Adams. "Be the Leader God Meant You to Be." Page 64)

The Heart of a Servant Provides Leadership That Changes Lives

A. Without a clear vision, people have no clear direction, so they go from Sunday to Sunday and soon lose a sincere passion for Christ. They keep looking for the high that comes from a great worship service rather than the joy that comes from serving God's people with a clear vision (Proverbs 29:18; Habakkuk 2:2-3).

B. Today the Lord is looking for people who care nothing for the empty praise or temporal pleasures of this world (Hebrews 11:24-29). He is seeking men and women who care that the world needs Christ and who are eager to follow Him with single-mindedness and purpose. A servant has a laser focus on serving the Lord for His glory and the blessings of those around them.

   1. Moses' single-mindedness made a difference and changed lives (Exodus 14:15-18, 21-24).

   2. Paul's single-mindedness dominated his ministry; "*We proclaim Him, admonishing every man and teaching every man with all wisdom, so that we may present every man complete in Christ. For this purpose, also I labor, striving according to His power, which mightily works within me.*" (Colossians 1:28-29)

C. Key ingredients that drive leaders to serve members who are on their team:

   1. Prayer for the personal needs of each individual in that particular ministry. The leader must keep up with the needs of

members in their ministry, and make sure they are cared for. When members from their group are sick or have lost a loved one, they should be the first to send a card or visit them. When a person feels that those whom they serve care for them, these individuals then serve with more dedication and commitment once they are strong again.

2. There are four dimensions that should be put in place when working with a small group:

  a. Personal (the individual)

  b. Spiritual (short devotionals)

  c. Social (the group)

  d. Production (accomplishing the task)

Service That Is Based on a Believer's Spiritual Gift

A. Everyone has a spiritual gift (1 Peter 4:10).

B. Spiritual gifts are for the building up of the body (Romans 12:3-8). It is a process that is continuously empowered by the ministry of the Holy Spirit.

C. When believers use their spiritual gifts, the church grows spiritually (Ephesians 4:13) and it functions more cohesively (Ephesians 4:16).

  1. Spiritual gifts, that are a result of the pastor equipping the saints (Ephesians 4:11), allow the body to do "work of service" (Ephesians 4:12).

  2. Spiritual gifts build up or edify [meaning promotes spiritual growth in the body; used figuratively for the building of a house with Christ as the chief cornerstone and the apostles writing as the foundation (Ephesians 2:19-22)] the members of the body of Christ in the following way:

a. We "all attain the unity of the faith."

b. "The knowledge of the Son of God."

c. Grow to spiritual maturity which is "the measure of the stature which belongs to the fullness of Christ."

d. The church is more unified because it is "fitted together fitly." (Ephesians 4:16).

D. Spiritual gifts when applied comprehensively, because each part is working (Ephesians 4:16; Romans 12:4), establishes the body of Christ's functionality on earth (Ephesians 1:22-23; 1 Corinthians 12:12), "who fills all in all." The benefits of the body of Christ functioning for God's glory is:

1. The *"gates of Hades shall not overpower it"* (Matthew 16:17).

2. The wisdom of God will be made known to the wicked (Ephesians 3:10).

3. We establish Christ's headship functionally (Ephesians 1:22-23; Colossians 1:16-20).

E. It is when believers use their spiritual gifts that they serve the common good of the body and expose the powerful work of the Trinity for the church. Then each member's life is impacted for the glory of God (1 Corinthians 12:4-27).

F. When a believer abides in God's Word and serves Him faithfully, they yield much fruit (John 15:1-5).

G. Spiritual gifts are powerful tools that God uses for all aspects of the church:

1. Elders must have the gift of knowledge and wisdom (Jeremiah 3:15). The gift of teaching is not required (1 Timothy 3:2; 'able to teach' — develop an ability to teach) but would be extremely useful.

2. Deacons must have the gift of service (Acts 6:1-6).

3. Ministers must have the gift of teaching and the gift of service (Ephesians 4:12; a minister is someone who served in a magistrate in a court of law. The disciples served Christ).

Conclusion

When the heart of a leader is truly shaped by the Spirit of God, God moves it to impact the heart of others. Without this, leadership is more about completing tasks than changing lives. The entire focus of the church is to disciple believers to be true worshipers of God. These believers, because their lives have been changed, will impact homes, communities, and the world. "The real test to your leadership is whether or not other leaders are developed as you lead the way. The development of Christlike character in the people for whom you are responsible is one of your prime objectives." (Jay Adams. "Be the Leader God Meant You to Be." Page 79)

CHAPTER 7

Constructing a Cohesive Leadership Team

Introduction

Developing an effective team to minister to the diverse needs of a church dominates how the church is organized throughout the New Testament. It is based on the reality that the church is the body of Christ. Like the human body, it is a coordinated, interwoven, and well-connected system that allows God's agenda to impact lives within the church, in the community, and around the world. *"From whom the whole body, being fitted and held together by what every joint supplies, according to the proper working of each individual part, causes the growth of the body for the building up of itself in love."* (Ephesians 4:16). As a matter of fact, after Paul discusses spiritual gifts, he says, *"**Now** you are Christ's body, and individually members of it."* (1 Corinthians 12:27).

Building a team of believers to serve based on their spiritual gifts provides a gateway for the Godhead to function powerfully. *"Now there are varieties of gifts, but the same Spirit. And there are varieties of ministries, and the same Lord. There are varieties of effects, but the same God who works all things in all persons. But to each one is given the manifestation of the Spirit for the common good."* (1 Corinthians 12:4-8)

It is a commitment to His standards that leads to unity. When each person is committed to use their spiritual gift for the glory of God

(1 Corinthians 12:4-8; one body), and each person is committed to demonstrate the love of God in and through their lives (Ephesians 4:16), Christ's prayers (John 17:20-23) are answered.

When these elements lead to unity then diversity serves to make the unified body a powerful experience which accomplishes God's purposes with a high level of efficiency.

This chapter will be divided into several sections. We will first focus on the significance of the pastor role and provide an outline written by Dr. Tony Evans, Pastor of Oak Cliff Bible Fellowship, a megachurch in Dallas, on his role. The second section outlines elders and how they work with the pastor, as well as their role. The third section outlines deacons and their role, and how they work with the pastor as well as how trustees work with the pastor and deacons to create a cohesive leadership body.

Building a Dynamic Team of Leaders

Key Principles to Bear in Mind as the Pastor, Elders, Deacons, and Possibly the Trustees Work Together:

1. These believers did not follow leaders because of their position, they followed leaders because those leaders were following Christ (Matthew 28:18-19). *"Be imitators of me, just as I also am of Christ."* (1 Corinthians 11:1; Hebrews 13:8)

2. Christ expects the pastor, elders, and deacons to take the work of the Holy Spirit very seriously (1 Timothy 4:16; Acts 20:28; Acts 6:2-3).

    a. Trusting in the influence of the Holy Spirit (John 14-16).

    b. Seals our salvation (14:16).

    -   *Guides us into truth* (14:16; 16:13).

    -   *We will have the ability to experience God* (14:20).

    -   *Establishes the love of God for us and in us* (14:21, 23-24).

- *Provides us the ability to recall the Word of God* (14:26).

- *Convicts us of sin* (16:7-11).

- *Provides us the fruit of the Spirit* (Galatians 5:22-25). *The fruit of the Spirit includes love, peace, and longsuffering.*

- *Illuminates the Word so that we can be able to teach* (1 Corinthians 2:10-15).

- *Provides us wisdom* (Jeremiah 3:15; Colossians 1:9-10). *Elders are to lead with wisdom.*

c. Remaining under the influence of the Holy Spirit causes us to be empowered to guide believers to Christ so that unity is maintained throughout the body (John 14:16).

- *Abide in His Word* (John 15; 17:13-19).

- *Christ prayed for unity* (John 17:20-24). <u>A lack of unity, as a result of changing what was agreed upon, in the case of Peter, led to division.</u>

d. When we are not in the Spirit there is <u>no unity</u> because the flesh is *"strife, jealousy, outbursts of anger, disputes, dissensions, factions, envying"* (Galatians 5:20-21). The scripture is clear about how to manage dissension:

- *"Now I urge you, brethren, keep your eye on those who cause dissensions and hindrances contrary to the teaching which you learned, and turn away from them. For such men are slaves, not of our Lord Christ but of their own appetites; and by their smooth and flattering speech they deceive the hearts of the unsuspecting."* (Romans 16:17-19)

- *"If anyone does not obey our instruction in this letter, take special note of that person and do not associate with him, so that he will be put to shame. Yet do not regard him as an enemy, but admonish him as a brother."* (2 Thessalonians 3:14-15)

- *"Reject a factious man after a first and second warning, knowing that such a man is perverted and is sinning, being self-condemned."* (Titus 3:10-11)

- When there is division the Pastors are held accountable, through the scriptures, to work hard to maintain the unity of the church:

  » *"But in case I am delayed, I write <u>so that you will know</u> how one <u>ought to conduct himself</u> in the household of God, which is the church of the living God, the pillar and support of the truth."* (1 Timothy 3:15-16)

  » *"For there are many rebellious men, empty talkers and deceivers, especially those of the circumcision, who must be silenced because they are upsetting whole families, teaching things they should not teach for the sake of sordid gain. One of themselves, a prophet of their own, said, 'Cretans are always liars, evil beasts, lazy gluttons.' This testimony is true. For this reason reprove them severely so that they may be sound in the faith, not paying attention to Jewish myths and commandments of men who turn away from the truth. To the pure, all things are pure; but to those who are defiled and unbelieving, nothing is pure, but both their mind and their conscience are defiled. They profess to know God, but by their deeds they deny Him, being detestable and disobedient and worthless for any good deed."* (Titus 1:10-16)

  » *"But avoid worldly and empty chatter, for it will lead to further ungodliness, and their talk will spread like gangrene. Among them are Hymenaeus and Philetus, men who have gone astray from the truth saying that the resurrection has already taken place, and they upset the faith of some. Nevertheless, the firm foundation of God stands, having this seal, 'The Lord knows those who are His,' and, 'Everyone who names the name of the Lord is to abstain from wickedness.'"* (2 Timothy 2:16-19)

Section I
A Biblical Outline of Pastor's God-Given Role

General Overview

Due to the vast nature of a pastoral position (a Biblical outline of this is provided below), the ministry of deacons plays a significant role in the overall development of the church (Exodus 18:19-23; Numbers 11:10-18; Acts 6:1-6; 1 Timothy 3:1-15). This comes as a result of the diverse needs of God's sheep and the work that Christ has ordained the church to do.

An example of this can be seen by the manner in which the God-head functions. This process demonstrates how God the Father, God the Son, and God the Holy Spirit powerfully care for the diverse needs of all creation. Understanding this process may serve as a model in directing the leadership of the local church while effectively nurturing the diverse needs of God's sheep. This helps the believers to progressively mature into the fullness of Christ.

The role of God the Father, God the Son, and God the Holy Spirit towards the church is an illustration of how God cares for the spiritual and physical needs of each believer. God provides the direction for the development of humankind (Genesis 12:1-3; John 3:16; Ephesians 1:11). Christ provides the means by which human's spiritual life is established based on God's plan (Genesis 3:15; John 1:1; Ephesians 1:7-10; Colossians 1:15-18).

The Holy Spirit is Christ's Helper just like Christ was and is God's Helper (John 14:16-17). The Holy Spirit provides direction (John 16:13), comfort (John 14:25-27), gives victory over the attacks of Satan (1 John 4:4), and power in our daily prayer life (Romans 8:26), so that we can do *"all things through Christ* (since the Holy Spirit is His Helper) *who strengthens us"* (Philippians 4:13). We are able to do all things because of the fruit of the Spirit (Galatians 5:22-24). This process allows us to do exactly what Adam did, and that is we can walk in step with the Spirit (Galatians 5:25) and allow Christ to accomplish the goal of His death on Calvary (2 Corinthians 3:18). This Trinitarian process is transferred to the church in two ways: (1) the leadership structure (1 Timothy 3:1-15) and (2) in the use of spiritual gifts (1 Corinthians 12:4-8).

The pastor is God's representative to the people (Exodus 18:19; Jeremiah 3:15) and must be called by God for this position (Ephesians 4:11). The pastor is gifted by God to teach the Word of God to His people (Exodus 18:20; 1 Timothy 4:11; 2 Timothy 4:2-3). *"I solemnly charge you in the presence of God and of Christ Jesus, who is to judge the living and the dead, and by His appearing and His kingdom: preach the word; be ready in season and out of season; reprove, rebuke, exhort, with great patience and instruction."* (2 Timothy 4:1-2) It is the scriptures that *"equips the man of God for every good work"* (2 Timothy 3:17). This is why the pastor is to study to show himself approved *"a workman not ashamed."* (2 Timothy 2:14). The pastor must develop the church's vision and show the members the way so that they become involved in God's kingdom work (Exodus 18:20; Ephesians 4:12). The pastor must also oversee the appointment of leaders (2 Timothy 2:2; Titus 1:5) and ensure that the church functions in an orderly manner (1 Timothy 3:15). Setting up the church to function orderly has more to do with a leadership structure than anything else. If this is not done a pastor will wear out (Deuteronomy 1:9-15). This is an administration that is suitable for the fullness of times (Ephesians 1:9-11).

Deacons must have wisdom (Acts 6:3), which is something someone prays for (James 1:5-8), and it comes after knowledge and understanding are applied (Colossians 1:9-10). However, deacons oversee the physical needs of the body as each believer lives out the Biblical principles that are taught primarily by the pastor and sometimes by elders (Acts 6:2-4; 1Timothy 3:8-13).

By developing this system of leadership, the kingdom work of God is re-established within the local church (Ephesians 1:22-23). Through this process, each believer is functionally challenged to grow and to mature (Ephesians 4:12-13; Colossians 1:28-29; Hebrews 13:7). It also provides believers a living example of spiritual maturity that they observe (Matthew 28:19) because their spiritual, as well as their physical, life is being nurtured. The development of a Biblical leadership structure becomes crucial to the effectiveness and strength of the church (1 Timothy 3:15). The importance of this structure is highlighted when Moses became frustrated and upset with God when the Israelites became tired of eating the same food day after day (Numbers 11:16-17).

In Numbers 11, the people wanted meat rather than the same diet God had provided. God came to Moses and told him to gather the elders and officers that he knew to be faithful and to bring them before Him at the tent of meeting. Once Moses completed the task he was instructed to do, God said, *"I will come down and speak with you there"* (Numbers 11:17). Notice that God did not say I will come down and speak with everyone. He said He would come down and speak with Moses. This is because Moses needed to share the load (Exodus 18:18). Even though leaders are in place to provide leadership, they must share the pastor's load that God has placed on them, as they endeavor to faithfully serve God. "Leadership begins with one person — the leader. A dozen management skills may be exercised, but ultimately the leadership equation may be reduced to a lone person, one individual whom people follow."[2]

Someone must explain the mind of God to the people (Exodus 18:19). There are those who must ensure that the principles taught are implemented into the lives of the people as well as into the life of the body (Exodus 18:21-22). Someone must ensure that the physical needs of the people are effectively served (Numbers 11:16; officers). This process serves as a blessing for the kingdom of God and strengthens the lives of His people. *"If you do this thing and God so commands you, then you will be able to endure, and all these people also will to their place in peace."* (Exodus 18:23). These individuals make up the church's leadership.

Explaining the mind of God is the pastor's responsibility with assistance from the elders. Serving the physical needs of the community is the deacons' responsibility (Acts 6:3-6). This structure was estab-

---

2   Myra, H. L. 1987. *Vol. 12: Leaders: Learning leadership from some of Christianity's best.* "A Leadership/Word book." The Leadership library. Christianity Today; Word Books: Carol Stream, Ill.; Waco, Tex.

lished by a foundation that was laid by the apostles with Christ Jesus as its cornerstone (1 Corinthians 3:10; Ephesians 2:20). This structure is implemented into a system that is empowered by each believer who has been given spiritual gifts through the ministry of the Holy Spirit for the proper operation of the body of Christ for the glory of God (1 Corinthians 12:4-8). *"As each one has received a special gift, employ it in serving one another as good stewards of the manifold grace of God."* (1 Peter 4:10)

This process is powerful because it provides Christ the opportunity to functionally operate as the head of the church (provided everyone is willing to allow the Word of God to control how the church operates), and the body to be shaped by ministries outlined in His Word (1 Corinthians 12:4-8; 12-31). When the world experiences the church as a viable organism, lives are powerfully impacted for the glory of God (Ephesians 1:22-23).

The plans for a leadership structure in the church, which has been examined and explained, is based on a Biblical system prescribed by the head of the church, Christ. This is why the planning and developmental process bathed with Scripture is so crucial. Therefore, the critiquing from anyone forces an exegetical response rather than a philosophical or denominational assessment.

Pastoral Leadership — An Introduction

It is clear in scripture that the primary role of the pastor is to provide the vision and strategy for the church (Exodus 18:17-20; Acts 20:27; Ephesians 4:12). He is to also provide direction or care concerning the major issues of the church (Exodus 18:22) and be the primary proclaimer for the teaching of God's Word (1 Timothy 5:17). It is important for members to experience the pastor functioning as the primary leader of the church just as it was when Moses led the people through the wilderness (even though Aaron and Joshua were present). Joshua led the people into the Promised Land, Peter led the disciples, and Paul led the process of impacting the Gentiles.

The role and responsibilities of a pastor are extremely important for the development and proper functioning of the local church. The pastor is responsible for many things. He leads by example, preaches and teaches, develops ministries, disciples and trains leaders to function in their Biblically prescribed roles, oversees the discipline of members and the overall welfare of the church, and oversees the spiritual development of each member. All these responsibilities and more are significant to the ongoing development of the church.

The Biblical Need (Pastor) for a Primary Leader in the Church

1. Moses was the primary leader in Israel and was responsible for serving as God's representative between God and the people. He was responsible for overseeing the other leaders and making key decisions regarding the direction God's people should go (Exodus 18:13-17).

2. God passed the primary leadership role of Israel from Moses to Joshua whose job it was to continue leading the people in God's way (Deuteronomy 34:9; Joshua 1:1-9).

3. The absence of a primary leader in Israel led to chaos among God's people (Judges 17:6, 21:25).

4. The primary leadership role of the school of the prophets and the nation of Israel, in general, was passed from Elijah to Elisha (2 Kings 2:12-15).

5. When Eli died, Samuel was appointed as the primary leader of Israel (1 Samuel 3; 12:1-2).

6. Jesus recognized Peter as the primary leader of the apostles (Matthew 16:15-19; John 21:15-17).

7. Paul sent Timothy and Titus to be the primary leaders in Ephesus and Crete and gave them the authority to exercise that role (1 Timothy 3:15; Titus 1:5).

8. Each of the <u>seven churches of Revelation had a primary leader</u> whose responsibility it was to deliver Christ's message to the church. (Revelation 2-3; "the angel of the church" is a reference to pastor based on Galatians 4:14; 1 Timothy 5:21).

9. **Jesus Christ is the Chief Shepherd and He has appointed other Shepherds** (Jeremiah 3:15; Ephesians 4:11; Colossians 1:7; 1 Peter 5:1-5) to disciple believers (Matt. 28:19-20), in an effort to further the work Christ started (Ephesians 1:21-22). This focus called for the development of unique men who will in total obedience and submission respond to Christ's direction.

10. In Numbers 11:16-17, when God instructed Moses to get elders and officers God specifically stated, *"The Lord therefore said to Moses, 'Gather for Me seventy men from the elders of Israel, whom <u>you know</u> to be the elders of the people and their officers and bring them to the tent of meeting, and let them take their stand there <u>with you</u>. Then I will come down and <u>speak with you</u> there, and I will take of the Spirit who <u>is upon you</u>, and will put Him upon them; and they shall bear the burden of <u>the people with you</u>, so that you will <u>not bear it all alone.</u>'"*

11. After talking to Timothy about the qualifications of elders and deacons Paul writes, *"I am writing <u>these things to you</u>, hoping to come to you before long; but in case I am delayed, I write so that you will know how one ought to conduct himself in the household of God, which is the church of the living God, the pillar and support of the truth."* (1 Timothy 3:14-16) Paul also instructs Timothy to, *"Prescribe and teach these things. Let no one look down on your youthfulness, but rather in speech, conduct, love, faith and purity, show yourself an example to those who believe."* (1 Timothy 4:11-12)

12. Paul instructed Titus in the same manner. *"These things speak and exhort and repose with all authority. Let no one disregard you."* (Titus 2:15)

The Biblical Responsibilities of the Pastor

Some of the principles shared are taken from an outline provided by Dr. Anthony Evans.

1. The pastor/teacher is to be the primary proclaimer of the scriptures for the church (Jeremiah 3:15; 2 Timothy 4:2; Titus 1:5-9). This is accomplished through preaching the Word at church services and teaching church leaders on a regular basis.

2. He establishes the vision for the church (Exodus 18:20; Numbers 11:17; Ephesians 4:12).

3. The pastor/teacher oversees the orderly operation of the church (Titus 1:5). This is accomplished through overseeing the coordination of the ministries of the church through the leaders.

4. The pastor/teacher oversees the appointment of the church leadership (Titus 1:5). This is accomplished through ensuring that the constitution guidelines for appointing church leaders are followed.

5. The pastor/teacher oversees the financial welfare of church leadership (1 Timothy 5:17-18). Ensuring that policies are in place and followed for counting the church's funds, proper purchasing policies are in place, and accounting procedures are properly followed accomplish this.

6. The pastor/teacher oversees the training of leaders (2 Timothy 2:2). This is accomplished through regular Bible study with the leaders and special leadership retreats and workshops. This also includes developing training material for newly appointed elders and deacons.

7. The pastor/teacher oversees the discipline of leaders (1 Timothy 3:9-10). This is accomplished through ensuring that the constitutional guidelines for the discipline of leaders are followed.

8. The pastor/teacher oversees the overall welfare of the whole church (1 Timothy 3:15). This is accomplished by regularly meeting with all

leadership to ensure that the scripture is the standard that governs their beliefs and actions as well as making sure the guidelines of the church are functioning properly in the life of the membership.

9. The pastor should be an <u>ex-officio member of each and every board, council, and committee of the church.</u>

Pastoral Leadership as It Relates to Elders

There is a need for this body to function as a unified body:

1. *"I know that after my departure savage wolves will come in among you, not sparing the flock; and from among your own selves men will arise, speaking perverse things, to draw away the disciples after them. Therefore be on the alert, remembering that night and day for a period of three years I did not cease to admonish each one with tears. And now I commend you to God and to the word of His grace, which is able to build you up and to give you the inheritance among all those who are sanctified."* (Acts 20:29-33)

2. *"For our struggle is not against flesh and blood, but against the rulers, against the powers, against the world forces of this darkness, against the spiritual forces of wickedness in the heavenly places."* (Ephesians 6:12-13;)

Sustaining a Cohesive Leadership Process

These guidelines can be used for a structure where there are no elders, only deacons.

1. When decisions are being made, they have to be made with a deep commitment to the following principles:

    a. The Word of God must be dominant.

    b. Must commit to carefully read through all documents provided and work within the elders' meetings for a clear understanding.

    c. Work through the decision process with a commitment to achieve unity.

    d. All discussions concerning the decisions take place <u>only</u> in elders' meetings. No sidebars during the week through phone calls or in parking lots.

    e. Seek to remain within the policies, doctrinal statement, position papers, and by-laws of the church.

2. Elders need to agree to be committed to the leadership structure of the church.

3. Once there is a majority vote everyone has to agree to faithfully get behind the decision whether they voted for or against it:

    a. This includes the signing of documents.

    b. Standing for the decision if the decision requires a congregational vote.

    c. Financially supporting the decision if it requires that.

    d. Maintaining a positive and supportive voice among congregants.

4. Work together to fight (1 Timothy 6:12), within Biblical guidelines, against divisive activities (Romans 16:17-18; 2 Thessalonians 3:14-15; Titus 3:10-11; 1 Peter 3:13-17) among leadership or the church while protecting the church against wolves (Acts 20:25-31).

5. Once church discipline issues are decided, elders agree to function as a cohesive unit to manage the issue while protecting the church against division.

The Pastor Is Accountable for the Following to the Elders' Ministry

1. Finances – Once the vision is outlined and designed, a budget is correlated to it. Once the budget is outlined, it is brought to the

elders for a vote before it goes for a congregational vote (1 Timothy 5:17-18).

2. Ordination – all leaders and ministers are always collectively ordained (1 Timothy 4:14; 2 Tim 1:6).

3. Appointment of elders or deacons – The pastor can select individuals to be elders and deacons (1 Timothy 3:1-2; 5:22; Titus 1:5). He needs to bring these individuals to the elders for final approval (Acts 14:23; Acts 15).

4. Church Discipline – These issues are determined collectively (Matthew 18:15-20; 1 Timothy 5:17-19)

5. Doctrine – The discussion for Paul to go to the Gentiles was a collective decision (Acts 15) but before these leaders met, God gave Peter a vision to go to Cornelius so that Peter can provide leadership in resolving this issue. The best way to approach this is to have the pastor write a paper on the issue and present to the elders.

6. Formation of church policies

7. Purchase of buildings, vans, or getting loans – your by-laws may address this.

8. Affiliation with other organizations – Paul going to the Gentiles (Acts 15).

9. Praying for the sick (James 5:14-15).

10. Guarding the church against wolves (Acts 20:28-31).

11. The pastor cannot hold the office of treasurer or secretary.

When Elders Disagree with the Pastor's Decision

"Do not receive an accusation against an elder except on the basis of two or three witnesses. Those who continue in sin, rebuke in the presence of all, so that the rest also will be fearful of sinning. I solemnly charge you in the presence of God and of Christ Jesus and of His chosen angels, to maintain

these principles without bias, doing nothing in a spirit of partiality." (1 Timothy 5:19-21)

1. If the decision made is an area that is not listed from 1–11 above, then the elders must prayerfully come under the pastor's leadership since God has called him to be the primary leader (outlined in this chapter "The Biblical Need (Pastor) for a Primary Leader in the Church"). This continually allows the church to remain cohesive. A few examples – time of worship services, moving to two services, selecting ministry leaders, just to name a few.

2. If it comes to an area the pastor is accountable to the elders for, as the elders seek to respect pastoral leaders, here are some guidelines that may be of assistance:

    a. When it comes to two or three witnesses approaching an elder it is the same process as Matthew 18:15-20. It has to be based on facts and it must serve the purpose of winning your brother back.

    b. When there was Disagreement of Paul being called by God to go to the elders, the following took place. This is exemplified in Acts 15:1-2, *"Some men came down from Judea and began teaching the brethren, 'Unless you are circumcised according to the custom of Moses, you cannot be saved.' And when Paul and Barnabas had great dissension and debate with them, the brethren determined that Paul and Barnabas and some others of them should go up to Jerusalem to the apostles and elders concerning this issue."*

        i. These men did not move forward until *"…it seemed good to the apostles and the elders, with the whole church, to choose men from among them to send to Antioch with Paul and Barnabas — Judas called Barsabbas, and Silas, leading men among the brethren, and they sent this letter with them…."* (Acts 15:22)

        ii. When Peter stepped away from this, Paul held him accountable publicly because Peter broke the agreement of the elders and apostles publicly. *"But when Cephas came to Antioch,*

I opposed him to his face because he stood condemned." (Galatians 2:11-14) <u>Paul did this because when the issue is over it is over. Nothing can be changed from what everyone decided when everyone was together, even if this is Peter the person who God called to lead the disciples</u> (Matthew 16:17-18). Remember that in their day there was no email or phones, so when the meeting is over it is literally over because they are called to travel into the world (Acts 1:8).

Section II
A Biblical Outline of the Role of Elders

General Guidelines

1. As in the case of the pastor, elders need to remember that a title does not make them elders. It is <u>their spiritual growth</u> and <u>function</u> that shapes them to be the leaders God has called them to be.

   a. *"Be on guard for yourselves and for all the flock, among which the **Holy Spirit has made you overseers**, to shepherd the church of God which He purchased with His own blood."* (Acts 20:28)

   b. When we obey the Word of God to operate as elders we choose to abide in God (John 15:1-10), and we do not end up in the flesh (Galatians 5:16-21). The flesh does not lead to us *"inheriting the kingdom of God"*—the Holy Spirit (Ephesians 1:14). **This is why obeying a Biblical structure is essential to spiritual growth, the health of the elder's ministry and the strength of the church. It is not just about a structure; it is about reverencing God's structure in the manner in which we submit to His Word. When the church body sees this example, that is when they are charged to follow us (Hebrews 13:7,17).**

   c. *"Remember those who led you, who spoke the word of God to you; <u>and considering the result of their conduct, imitate their faith.</u>*

Jesus Christ is the same yesterday and today and forever." (Hebrews 13:7-8) Christ remained the same because the leaders were faithful. Imitating faith is built on Hebrews 11. Obedience and trust in God for His Word (Hebrews 11:6). All leaders must view the Word of God as:

- *Truth* (1 John 1:1-2; 2 Peter 1:16-21), *therefore we must be committed to renew or minds* (Romans 12:2).

- *Sufficient* (Hebrews 1:4; 2 Timothy 3:12-16).

- *Powerful* (Hebrews 4:12).

- *Everlasting* (1 Peter 1:23-25).

2. The need for spiritual growth means that an elder must be involved in the following:

   a. Bible study.

   b. Worship.

   c. Elders' meetings.

   d. Elders' and deacons' meetings.

   e. Leadership training — general sessions — and continuing education blesses everyone.

   f. Prayer meeting or church revivals.

The Role of the Pastor as it Relates to Elders

General Overview

1. Before the time of Exodus 18 when there was Abraham, Isaac, and Jacob, Melchizedek (Genesis 14:18-19) and Jethro, who was a high priest before God (Moses' father-in-law), were elders (Genesis 50:7; Ex 3:16, 18; 4:29; 12:21; 17:5-6). These individuals were key leaders in God's administration.

2. Elders always function in the role as advisors, men of wisdom, or interpreters of the law as we would see the case of Boaz in Ruth 4:2; Job 12:20.

3. God gave them the gift of wisdom and knowledge (Jeremiah 3:15) not the gift of leadership.

4. Elders functioned in the midst of the Levitical system where there were High Priests and Levites. They were also functioning during the time of the Pharisees, Sadducees, and Zealots. They were not the main leaders even in this system. It was the High Priest or kings.

5. Elders in this system were interpreters of the law (Mark 7:6).

6. In the midst of the meeting of the apostles (these were key leaders and the ones who God use to lay the foundation for the New Testament church — Ephesians 2:20) and elders, Peter was the one Christ selected to reveal the truth to, allowing him to provide key leadership at a very key time in the development of the New Testament church (Acts 10:9-34, 44-48; Acts 11:17-18; 15:6-14,19).

7. When elders were appointed in every city by Paul and Barnabas it did not say that they were now leading the churches (Acts 14:23 – there is not much said because they were dealing with Peter who already knew how elders functioned). I believe that the example of how they function in the very next chapter provides us an example of their role, which was to work with key leaders in deciding doctrine and church policy.

8. In the case of 1 Peter 5:2, Paul who Peter knew about (2 Peter 3:15-16) writes after Paul and knows of the writings of Paul and says they are writings that are from God (1st and 2nd Timothy were written between AD 63-65 and AD 66-67, respectively).

Elder Responsibilities

1. I believe that it leads to a productive cohesive leadership structure for the church when the pastor serves as the chairman of the elders' ministry. For all the reasons stated above, including the things the pastor is accountable for, it is less confusing to have the pastor lead in this manner. To have the pastor as the primary leader and also have a chairman can create confusion, especially for a young Christian and new member who is still learning the polity of the church.

2. Assist the pastor in ensuring the church operates in accordance with sound Biblical principles and the policies and guidelines in the church constitution.

3. Assist in providing strong oversight by creating policy and approving administrative practices which ensure the spiritual growth of the elders, the pastor/teacher, deacons, church leadership, and membership.

4. To act as fellow disciples and also the group that the pastor/teacher is professionally accountable to (list provided above).

5. To assist the pastor in overseeing the overall process of discipleship in the church.

6. To assist the pastor in providing the church with protection against negative influences.

7. To teach against errant doctrine.

8. To discipline errant believers.

9. To give leadership to address the moral and spiritual issues facing the church.

10. To assist the pastor in selecting men and women of the high spiritual qualifications to become elders (Acts 14:23).

11. To select men and their wives to serve as deacons.

12. To define the character, scope, and nature of all church organizational relationships. This includes internal church organizations and the church's relationship with external organizations, affiliated and unaffiliated.

13. Each elder that serves as vice chairman, treasurer, or secretary is responsible for carrying out their duties as outlined in this document.

14. Some elders can also assist in the overseeing of ministry development and new member classes. This allows the elders an opportunity to teach and to protect the flock from wolves that may come in among them (Acts 20:27-30).

15. Serve as spiritual leader over a group of assigned deacons.

16. Attend the elders' meeting each month. One is for spiritual issues, the other is for business-related items.

Section III
A Biblical Outline of the Role of Deacons

General Overview

The office of deacon/deaconess embodies the concept of serving in the church. The Greek word "*diakonos*" is translated as servant (sometimes slave) and is used to refer to the office of deacon/deaconess. There are several illustrations in the New Testament of being appointed to specific functions to serve the temporal and physical needs of the church. One of the best pictures of servanthood is found in Acts 6:1-6. It is questionable whether this passage refers to the office of deacon, but it certainly illustrates service to the church. Those who model this kind of service are vital parts of the ministry of the church.

The role of deacons is distinctively outlined by the Apostles in Acts 6:1-6. This is because the Apostles had a lot of widows who were not being taken care of. It was apparently taking time away from their role which is to study and teach the scriptures. As stated in the opening section, God is seeking to care for His flock spiritually and physically. The deacons care for God's flock physically so technically they do not have a governing role even though that is the case in most Baptist churches. As a result, I would suggest that the deacon ministry in those cases be divided into the following:

1. Administrative Deacons – These are deacons who have the gift of service but also have the gift of administration. These deacons can form an executive committee that meets with the pastor for the governance of the church. I believe that it is best for the pastor to serve as the chairman for all the reasons listed above. However, it would be wise to have a deacon coordinator who works with the pastor to help coordinate meetings and all the upkeep that takes place in manage the deacon board (Baptist Church) or in the case where there are elders, deacons.

   a. These deacons can also oversee the counting of the offering (I don't believe they have to count it because there are many trustworthy people that can help in this area as well as those who work in accounting or maybe CPAs).

   b. These deacons can also help, if there is no janitor or maintenance crew, to open and close the church.

   c. These deacons can also help with security, especially on Sunday morning.

2. Family Deacons – These deacons have the gift of service and mercy. The focus of this ministry is to consistently remain in touch with the families of the church. It is to also minister to the needs of families whether they are sick and shut in, hospitalized, have problems paying bills (they are referred to the Benevolent Committee), have family members who have died, etc. It is an effort to build long-lasting relationships with families that would stimulate them, because they are cared for, to grow spiritually.

3. Ministry Deacons – These are deacons who have the gift of service but may also have the gift of teaching, like in the case of Stephen. These deacons, along with the ministers, can assist the pastor with overseeing the implementation of the vision into the life of the church.

Deacons' Ministry Function

1. To serve the church by giving leadership in addressing the temporal and material needs of the body.

2. To be available to serve in all services, as necessary, involving the corporate body.

3. Be prepared to serve in Communion and Baptism services.

4. To ensure that each member of the church body is accountable and accounted for (Colossians 1:28-29).

5. To assist in providing protection for the church against negative influences.

    a. To assist in the identification of errant doctrine in the church.

    b. To assist in the discipline and restoration of errant believers.

    c. To provide personal and moral leadership in some of the critical issues facing the church.

    d. Members or leaders who are functioning in a divisive manner.

6. Assist in the administering and giving funds to those who are in need through the Benevolence Fund.

7. To care for the assigned families based on the family ministry, making the contacts as outlined by this ministry. Each deacon will be assigned a family (ideally ten to fifteen families) that is in their geographical location. The deacon will have an elder to report to on a monthly basis. The deacon and the elder can partner in re-

sponding to some of the needs of the families. This may start out with a call at the church office. The deacon must talk directly with the church secretary.

a. If it is the member who called in, then the church secretary is responsible to call the deacon for that particular area.

b. The deacon will contact the family, and after meeting them, will make an assessment of the issue.

c. If the person is:

- **In the hospital**, the deacon will call the Comfort and Care Coordinator to assist them **(this will only occur if the deacon has more than one person sick at the same time or the person will be in the hospital for an extended period of time).** The deacon will then contact the elder to let them know. The deacon will seek to visit the family at least once during their hospital stay and then follow-up with a call after they get home or ask the Comfort and Care Coordinator to call the family if the deacon has more than one family in the hospital. The Comfort and Care Coordinator or their assistant will make sure that flowers were sent to the hospital for the family (this ministry will be discussed later).

- **Dealing with financial problems,** the deacon will contact the benevolent ministry. The deacons will follow-up with the family to make sure they were cared for.

- **Having serious problems**, whether marital or otherwise, the deacon will contact the elder they are assigned to. In the case where there are no elders, they contact the pastor. Major issues can include:

  » Divorce
  » Separation
  » Spousal abuse
  » Major surgery
  » Emotional distress and breakdown
  » Death of family member
  » Sudden job loss
  » Church discipline issues

- **In need of assistance in making decisions** or help in resolving some issues in their lives, the deacon can contact the pastor or counseling ministry. While visiting a family, a deacon should always take time to see if they have any questions about the church or anything else. If the deacon cannot answer, then the deacon should seek out the answer and provide it to the family. Whenever there is a prayer need, the deacon should note this on their form and let the prayer coordinator for the church know about this need. Deacons are to work with the assigned elder for accountability and support.

Section IV
Deacons and Trustees Working Cohesively

General Overview

It is extremely important to remember that the church is the body of Christ (Ephesians 1:22-23) and Christ is the head of the church (Colossians 1:15-18). The design and development of the church are based on the direction and influence of the Godhead; *"Now there are varieties of gifts, but the same Spirit. And there are varieties of ministries, and the same Lord. There are varieties of effects, but the same God who works all things in all persons. But to each one is given the manifestation of the Spirit for the common good."* (1 Corinthians 12:4-8) As a result, it is the responsibility of the leadership of the church to *"let all things be done properly and in an orderly manner."* (1 Corinthians 14:40) Paul instructs Timothy in 1 Timothy 3:15, *"I write so that you will <u>know how one ought to conduct himself in the household of God</u>, which is the church of the living God, the pillar and support of the truth."*

Trustees as a role is nowhere mentioned in the scriptures, which clearly states that God outlined the church with an *"administration suitable to the fullness of the times...."* (Ephesians 1:10) Trustees came into play because the government says that if a church dissolves, it needs a group of people they can work with to distribute the property of the church. There are particular tax regulations that must be adhered to as a religious non-profit, such as the church's assets properly going to another 501(c)(3) organization. God, who has a 'suitable administration,' has a leadership structure that can manage this. In the case where there are elders, it would be the elders (1 Timothy 5:17-18). If there are no elders, then the deacons, who God requires to be spiritual and wise (Acts 6:3), can best manage this since the church is not to rely on government to make its decisions (1 Corinthians 6:1-8).

1. This board (called a board in most Baptist churches) can constitute some difficulties for a church Biblically:

    a. The development of trustee board will constitute two functioning boards, two active chairmen, vice-chairmen, and the pastor in one institution.

    b. There are no Biblical guidelines or qualifications for this board, which means it will always be very difficult to hold this board accountable before a church.

    c. Because this board is most times made up of professionals, in the black community where there is not an over-abundance of professionals, their word, most of the time, carries a lot of weight, which sometimes overrides the authority of the deacon board and the pastor, two God-ordained bodies. The major concern with this is that most of these men and women are voted unto the board not because of their spiritual development but because of their professional capabilities. As a result, professionals make the decisions for the church rather than the pastor who is called to be the overseer of the church (1 Timothy 3:1-2, 15), and deacons who were called to be spiritual men, full of wisdom (Acts 6:3).

    d. The above process reverses the Biblical order for the decision making in the church. The final decision was given to the pastor with assistance from elders (Titus 2:15; 1 Timothy 3:15; Acts 6:1-6; 1 Peter 5:2,3; 1 Timothy 3:1,15; 3:9, 13) or, in a Baptist church, the pastor with the assistance of the deacons.

    e. It is better to develop a building or finance committee to handle the church property, the buying and selling of property, and the distribution of church funds under the direction of the pastor and deacon board, rather than to develop a whole new board.

    f. In reference to the requirements placed upon the church by the state, the deacon board can handle this. The Bible places this responsibility on the deacons by charging them to handle the physical matters of the church. Ephesians 1:9-11 says, *"He made known to us the mystery of His will, according to His kind intention which He purposed Him with a view to an administration suitable to the fullness of times, that is the summing up of all things in Christ, things in the heavens and things upon the earth."*

    g. There can be several subcommittees to the deacon ministry. For example, deacons who care for families in the church, deacons who handle the administrative needs of the church, deacons who care for benevolence, etc.

2.   I would suggest that no one serves on this board unless they meet these qualifications:

    a. The focus of all leadership must be as follows:

- Bring their lives under the conformity of God's Word (2 Timothy 3:12-16).

- Making disciples (Matthew 28:19-20).

- Present believers complete in Christ (Colossians 1:28-29).

    b. Leaders must lead by example:

- A leader must be a person of integrity at home, in society (blameless Ephesians 1:4), and at church (1 Timothy 3:4,5,12).

- Character and role are blended inseparably in ministry (1 Timothy 4:12; 2 Timothy 1:13; Hebrews 13:7-8).

3. Here is a process I would suggest so that the church functions in a cohesive manner:

    a. In order to maintain a cohesive process with the pastor as the chairman of the deacon board, it would be wise for trustees to work with the deacon coordinator so that the leadership structure of the church is delineated definitively. This process can operate in this manner:

        • Definition: "Trustees generally have the responsibility for maintaining and improving the church property, the handling of funds according to church budget and church authorization, and the buying and selling of property according to church authorization." (F. Massey Jr. and S.B. McKinney. "Administration in the Black Perspective." Page 80)

        • Guidelines for Operating the Trustee Board:

            » The budget that trustees manage is a budget that has been structured based on the pastor's vision for the church and a budget that is approved by the congregation.

            » The trustees review the budget to ensure that it remains within the agreed upon line items and that all the church's obligations are managed appropriately.

            » The church budget should be developed as a result of the pastor's vision or five-year plan in conjunction with the deacon board.

            » Any purchase or sale of property must follow the guidelines outlined in the church constitution. The decision to purchase property should be based on the pastor's vision and approved by the congregation. The trustee board does not approve this; they manage the acquisition.

            » The pastor and deacon board must approve any improvements done on the church property. The trustee board manages the improvement process.

» The trustee board assists the pastor with the maintenance of the property. This includes, but is not limited to, the day-to-day repairs.

- Some advantages to this board include that they allow the deacons the freedom to deal with ministering to the needs of the families in the church while they tend to those items outlined above.

Conclusion

Working together as a team for the glory of God was exemplified by Jesus and the disciples, Moses and his elders, Joshua and his elders (Joshua 1:3-10), and Paul and the elders of Ephesus (Acts 20:27-32). This was the prayer of Christ that leaders function in harmony with one another "*... that they may all be one; even as You, Father, are in Me and I in You, that they also may be in Us, so that the world may believe that You sent Me....*" (John 17:21) God leads the Godhead who function as one because they are committed to the same word and are obviously dominated by the same Spirit. Remember, "where there is unity there is strength."

Where there is righteousness, holiness, and perfection there is unity. It is when people function in the flesh that there is division and non-productivity. *"Now the deeds of the flesh are evident, which are: immorality, impurity, sensuality, idolatry, sorcery, enmities, strife, jealousy, outbursts of anger, disputes, dissensions, factions, envying, drunkenness, carousing, and things like these, of which I forewarn you, just as I have forewarned you, that those who practice such things will not inherit the kingdom of God."* (Galatians 5: 19-21)

The above verses clearly demonstrate that unity cannot be obtained where there is no structure. Even the Godhead though equal has structure (1 Corinthians 11:3; Philippians 2:6-11). This structure cannot be manmade because then the flesh will control it, which is destructive. It must be designed by the standards of God so that it is Spirit-empowered and -controlled.

CHAPTER 8

Creating and Implementing the Church's Vision as a Cohesive Leadership Team

Introduction

Over the years I have had the privilege of working with pastors and leaders across the country and in a few parts of the world. I have yet to meet a pastor who did not have some idea of what he wanted to see happen in the church God placed in his care. Some ideas were short-term and some were long-term plans. However, the process for outlining the vision statement and implementing a strategic plan with the cooperation of the church leadership was often a rocky course for some pastors.

Short-term plans such as building programs or the buying of vans, when accomplished, seemed to only create a need for more plans, and more plans, and more plans, which led to a lot of pressure and stress. The short-term patterns of reaching the goal and then the ensuing stress soon became the norm because it is very difficult to be a leader and to not know where one is going. To not have a progressive developmental process that evolves over a period of time focused on ministering to the needs of parishioners cause many churches to drift from one Sunday to another. This lack of a long-term direction tends to affect how the church building is built and how the church budget is outlined. Churches with short-term vision statements tend to wander from program to program. It is not that some of these pastors did not have a passion for a variety of things; they just did not meticulously carve out their vision (this word will be defined later) with a systematic plan outlining how they plan to implement their visions.

Some pastors struggle with elder or deacon boards to get their vision heard or supported. The pastor feels restrained because on one hand, the leaders want to know where the church is going and on the other hand, they struggle with supporting the pastor's ideas. Sometimes there are just one or two influential individuals on the board that disagree so strongly they cause others, who for sake the of peace or to not create division, stop discussing the issue and it soon dies. The pastor is then faced with going from Sunday to Sunday with no clear idea of a vision or who is leading the church. Some pastors, for the sake of their families, decide to preach, teach, counsel, and care for the sick and pray for church growth. Growing the church is important because if the pastor does not create church growth this whole process begins all over again. Questions such as, where are we going? Why are people leaving? Why is no one developing a clear direction for the church? end up directed at the pastor, even though he is not allowed to lead. Many pastors become disillusioned and begin looking for greener pastures. The members then become disillusioned and even though they wonder why pastors are not staying long, they do little to help turn things around.

Moses sent out spies to the Promised Land (Numbers 13). These spies were courageous to go throughout the land that God had prepared for them. They were committed. They stayed until they had good understanding of what was in the land. There was no question that Moses was God's called leader. God presented this visibly to the people daily (Exodus 33:7-12). There was no debate on what they were supposed to do and where they needed to go. They understood that they left Egypt to enter the land that was promised for over four hundred years. But when they saw difficulties ahead, these leaders persuaded the people to follow them rather than Moses and as a result, the people perished for a lack of vision (Proverbs 29:18). The people wandered for forty years without a vision and therefore, without meaning. A whole group of peopled died because leaders refused to follow God's vision that He presented through chosen leader.

Many, if not all, believers would agree that Christ died for the church and it is His shed blood that allows us all to be in His kingdom. Most believers would agree that Christ is the head of the church (Colossians 1:18) and the church is designed to a structure that represents Christ's body on earth (Ephesians 1:22-23; 1 Corinthians 12:4-7, 27). Members of the church and leaders would agree that God calls a pastor into ministry (Ephesians 4:11). He called a pastor but did not call elders or deacons. These are positions that leaders can desire, and Paul says, "*it is a fine work he desires to do.*" (1 Timothy 3:1) "*Therefore, brethren, select from among you...*" (Acts 6:3); Deacons were selected by the people.

It is only through the church that Christ accomplishes His plan for all mankind. "*And He put all things in subjection under His feet and gave Him as head over all things to the church.* (Ephesians 1:22) In Ephesians 3:10, Paul goes on to inform us that this is done "*in order that they manifold wisdom of God might now be made known through the church to the rulers and authorities in heavenly places.*" It is only through the church that Satan's gates can be locked or opened (Matthew 16:18-19). It is imperative that the pastor is given the freedom to develop God's plan for Christ's church. Please understand that as far as God is concerned, He has provided the plan: "*He made known to us the mystery of His will, according to His kind intention which He purposed in Him with a view to an administration suitable to the fullness of the times, that is, the summing up of all things in Christ, things in the heavens and things on the earth. In Him also we have obtained an inheritance, having been predestined according to His purpose who works all things after the counsel of His will, to the end that we who were the first to hope in Christ would be to the praise of His glory.*" (Ephesians 1:9-12)

Christ has also provided all the ministries of the church (easy to do since it is His body) and the Helper the Holy Spirit to accomplish the plan (1 Corinthians 12:4-7). It is of extreme importance that we address how leaders in the church lead and at the same time work with the pastor to develop a vision for the church. Many churches have died or just exist as a religious institution where people find friends, critique the pastor, his wife and children, and pray for those who despitefully use them. Many such churches struggle with church growth and they go from one Sunday to the next. No one is being baptized, no souls are being won, Bible study attendance is very low, and worship continues with the same songs and the same order of worship "that was sent from heaven" before the pastor even came on board.

The question is how does a leader move from great ideas to a productive process, which is implemented in such a manner that it forms a strategy that defines the nature and function of the church? Some of these key points are further developed in our resource, "Making Your Vision a Reality," available on our Power Walk Ministries website (www.powerwalkministries.org). In it, we are designed to provide are a systematic process to guide leaders to function in a cohesive manner for the vision statement to become a reality in the life of the church.

Designing the Vision Statement

A. Definition of a vision statement:

1. "Visionary planning is a process by which a church envisions its future and develops the necessary procedures and operations to achieve that future." — J. William Pfeiffer

2. "A visionary plan is a framework for carrying out strategic thinking, directions, and action leading to the achievement of consistent and planned results." — Patrick J. Below, George L. Morrisey, and Betty Acomb

B. Developing the vision statement as a Pastor:

1. No matter what is outlined in this process you must pray, pray, and pray again and again. As a pastor you are constantly seeking God for guidance.

2. Brainstorm. Include all the things you feel a strong desire to develop.

3. List where you feel the people are presently.

4. What are the passions for ministry that drive you as the pastor?

5. As the pastor you must evaluate your strengths and weakness.

6. What are the needs of the congregation?

7. What are the needs of the surrounding community and the city?

8. List all the present ministries and grade their effectiveness on a scale from 1-10.

9. Understand the changes that are occurring around you.

10. How will the changes made affect the church?

11. Are there enough people to help with the changes that need to be made?

12. What are the needs of the community?

13. There are three questions that must be answered. They are as follows:

    a. Why are we here? (Purpose — why?; vision — what?)

    b. Where are we going (What is the mission of the church?)

    c. How do we get to where we should be going? (What actions should we take to get there?)

C. Putting together the vision statement:

1. Formulate your research into a paragraph. Try to be as concise as possible.

2. Set it down for about a week and then come back to it. Fine tune it by carefully evaluating every word. Make sure the statements are action statements.

3. Put together a group of ministry leaders, some of the main leaders (elders or deacons, depending on your structure) of the church and seek to gain their thoughts about the paragraph you have fine-tuned.

4. Once you have gathered their thoughts, set the statement aside again and pray.

5. Come back to it in another week and make the statement even more concise.

D. Developing objectives from the vision statement. This leads to the creation of a mission statement:

1. This outlines specifically what you will do in order to implement the vision of the church.

2. This should lead you into your ministry development plan for the church.

3. It should include not just what you are planning to do presently, but also what you are planning to do futuristically.

Planning Process for the Implementation of the Pastor's Vision Where the Leadership Is Elders and Deacons

General Overview

The pastor needs to outline his vision or a five-year plan for the church. He must outline a strategy for the implementation of the vision during this five-year period. A preliminary budget should be presented because it will strategically outline the impact of the vision on the church's finances. This process is a general overview for the overall development of the vision.

A. The pastor needs to help all leaders by providing the Biblical process behind the vision statement.

B. The vision is shared with the elder board in a properly called meeting (if the pastor is not the chairman, the chairman puts this on the agenda for the meeting after a time of prayer and devotion).

The pastor must be prepared to entertain their questions. Once the vision has clear Biblical support, the elders should fully support the pastor (as in the case of Moses, going into the Promised Land. The elders must not allow fear to repeat history. When the vision does not violate the Word of God there should be no reason not to support it). The pastor should remain open to the suggestions of the elders concerning the fine-tuning of the vision statement or structure that he presented. If the vision does not violate God's Word, the elders should not make suggestions that change the original intent of the plans presented by the pastor.

C. The elders then assist the pastor by providing spiritual guidance for how the vision can impact the body. The fine-tuning of the implementation of vision is best done through ministers and ministry leaders. It allows them to get buy-in as their ideas become valued. When this occurs, their energy and excitement create momentum throughout the body.

D. The pastor must begin to teach and preach on this subject regularly. This needs to be after the elders (majority) see no Biblical contradictions and therefore support the vision and are in concurrence with the implementation process being communicated through the ministry groups. What I mean is the discipleship ministry committee, the Christian education committee, Sunday School, and the teachers meeting, etc.

E. The elders must then meet with the deacons that are assigned to them to explain and define the pastor's vision or the five-year plan. The suggestions of the deacons can be taken back to the elders for review. After this takes place, the elders must continue to assist in the development of the plan. All the deacons cannot be involved in the implementation process because their main function is to care for the families in the church and to help give direction in reference to the disbursement of the Benevolence Fund. However, the ministry deacons and, in some cases, the administration deacons can help.

F. The pastor should formulate meetings with ministry leaders in an effort to organize the development of the vision. Here is an example of how this process can be coordinated:

1. Ministry staff – this includes associate pastors on staff:

    a. This committee is made up of staff members who provide direction to the major ministry areas of the church. Each ministry leader must review the vision and general outline and make recommendations. These recommendations will be evaluated in meetings set up for the purpose of functionally implementing the vision.

    b. Each of these leadership meetings should start with devotions aimed at consistently developing ministers and ministry leaders spiritually.

    c. Their job once all of this is done is to meet with their ministers (non-staffed ministers) and ministry leaders to get their buy-in which in turn is brought back to the pastor for finalization. If there are major changes that do not necessarily change the major aspects of the vision, the pastor seeks to keep the elder informed.

    d. The elders should review updates from these meetings so that there are no surprises when the overall process is complete.

2. Ministers and Ministry Committee:

    a. Ministers and ministry committees will meet with ministry teams to gear up for the implementation of the vision.

3. Finance Committee:

    a. This committee is made of the church's financial secretary, church accountant, and members who have accounting backgrounds. These individuals will review the organizational development of the vision (put together under the pastor's direction by the ministry committee) and map out how this strategy will be sustained financially.

4. Casting the vision:

  a. When everyone is informed through these small groups, it is best for the pastor to call a leadership meeting to cast the vision.

  b. This needs to be a big deal. The congregation does not need to know as yet. Once everyone is on the same page, messages have been preached, and Bible study lessons have been taught, then the pastor can unveil the vision to the church. This can be done in the following manner:

    • The vision statement placed in the bulletin.

    • The vision statement can be placed on a banner in the foyer.

    • The Sunday sermon is totally focused on sharing the good news.

    • This can also be done in a specially called church business meeting.

  c. Things to remember when casting the vision:

    • Must be enthusiastic about the vision and allow your enthusiasm to be infectious.

    • Always speak positively about the vision.

    • Be patient and never get tired of explaining the vision to the membership.

    • Always explain it from a Biblical perspective.

    • Must speak with a strong sense conviction.

    • Develop a slogan or motto to help the members capture the vision.

- Make sure that the vision and ministry development is a part of the new membership curriculum.

- Teach and encourage the leaders to tell people in their ministry areas about the vision of the church.

- Spend time Biblically explaining the vision to these individuals.

- Develop a brochure that describes the church vision, the ministries, and the background information on the pastor.

Planning Process for the Implementation of the Pastor's Vision Where the Leadership Is Deacons and Trustees

General Overview

The pastor needs to outline his vision or a five-year plan for the church. He must outline a strategy for the implementation of the vision during this five-year period. A preliminary budget should be presented because it will strategically outline the impact of the vision on the church's finances. This process is a general overview for the overall development of the vision.

A. The pastor needs to help all leaders by providing the Biblical process behind the vision statement.

B. The vision is shared with the deacon board in a properly called meeting (if the pastor is not the chairman, the chairman puts this on the agenda for the meeting after a time of prayer and devotion). The pastor must be prepared to entertain their questions. Once the vision has clear Biblical support, the deacons should fully support the pastor (as in the case of Moses going into the Promised Land. The deacons must not allow fear to repeat history.). The pastor should remain open to the suggestions of the deacons concerning the fine-tuning of the vision statement or structure that he presented. If the vision does not violate God's Word, the deacons should not make suggestions that change the original intent of the plans presented by the pastor.

C. The deacons then assist the pastor by providing spiritual guidance for how the vision can impact the body. The fine-tuning of the implementation of vision is best done through ministers and ministry leaders. It allows them to get buy-in as their ideas become valued. When this occurs their energy and excitement create momentum throughout the body.

D. The pastor must begin to teach and preach on this subject regularly. This needs to be after the deacons (majority) see no Biblical contradictions and therefore support the vision and are in concurrence with the implementation process being communicated through the ministry groups. What I mean is the discipleship ministry committee, the Christian education committee, Sunday School, and the teachers meeting, etc.

E. All the deacons cannot be involved in the implementation process because their main function is to care for the families in the church and to help give direction in reference to the disbursement of the Benevolence Fund. However, the ministry deacons and, in some cases, the administration deacons can help.

F. The administration deacons must then begin meeting with the trustees to start carving out a budget (this would be based on the recommendation that the group of accounts etc. had outlined) so that it supports the implementation of the vision.

   1. The budget numbers are finalized once the ministries have had a chance to provide their input in the strategy meetings.

   2. The budget is then taken back to the deacons for a vote. Once a majority vote is obtained, the budget is finalized for presentation to the church body in a properly called business meeting.

G. The pastor should formulate meetings with ministers and ministry leaders in an effort to organize the development of the vision. Here is an example of how this process can be coordinated:

1. Ministry staff:

    a. This committee is made up of staff members (this may include associate pastors that are on staff) who provide direction to the major ministry areas of the church. Each minister (non-staff) and ministry leader must review the vision and general outline and make recommendations. These recommendations will be evaluated in meetings set up for the purpose of functionally implementing the vision.

    b. Each of these leadership meetings should start with devotions aimed at consistently developing ministry leaders spiritually.

    c. Their job once all of this is done is to meet with their ministry leaders to get their buy-in, which in turn is brought back to the pastor for finalization. If there are major changes that do not necessarily change the major aspects of the vision, the pastor seeks to keep the deacons informed.

    d. The deacons should review updates from these meetings so that there are no surprises when the overall process is complete.

2. Ministers and Ministry Committee:

    a. Ministry committees will meet with ministry teams to gear up for the implementation of the vision.

3. Casting the vision:

    a. When everyone is informed through these small groups, it is best for the pastor to call a leadership meeting to cast the vision.

    b. This needs to be a big deal. The congregation does not need to know as yet. Once everyone is on the same page, messages have been preached, and Bible study lessons have been taught, then the pastor can unveil the vision to the church. This can be done in the following manner:

- The vision statement placed in the bulletin.

- The vision statement can be placed on a banner in the foyer.

- The Sunday sermon is totally focused on sharing the good news.

- This can also be done in a specially called church business meeting.

Conclusion

The body of Christ is functionally complete on earth through the church (Ephesians 1:22-23) and is designed to withstand the attacks of Satan on God's children (Ephesians 3:10; 1 Corinthians 5:7-13; 1 Peter 4:17) as a testimony to the world. The pastor's role is significant because he provides both spiritual and physical guidance for the development of the body of believers who must function cohesively for God's glory (Ephesians 4:1-7, 11-16).

The pastor is the primary leader in this process (1 Timothy 3:15; Titus 2:15). His leadership is transferred spiritually by the discipleship of leaders and functionally through the elders, deacons, ministers, and ministry leaders in the church. As a result, a pastor must seek to prepare himself spiritually and Biblically for the work of the ministry (2 Timothy 3:16-17) and develop leadership skills that will nurture believers to function for the glory of God.

CHAPTER 9

Leadership Delegating Responsibilities for Effective Ministry Development

Introduction

In many ministries people who demonstrate a desire to serve are given ministry responsibilities quickly, often without training, clearly defined expectations, or even any visible applicable skill sets required to do the job. I understand that there are so many needs in most ministries that finding help and keeping help is a constant pressure. Yet when responsibilities are delegated in this manner people become disillusioned, burned out, or they create confusion and can become disruptive.

The delegation of responsibilities for the effective development of a ministry requires several aspects. There must be the recruitment of qualified leaders, discipleship, effective training for the proper development of ministry gifts or talents, the development of a strategic process, and accountability.

These elements must be implemented so that people are not given a task they cannot complete. When these elements are not in place individuals who are not committed to the Lord do things that can be damaging to the ministry. A strategic process must be in place or individuals that are given a task function aimlessly. Where there is no accountability, people are not challenged to grow to become an effective part of the team.

Christ delegated responsibilities to His disciples but it was after much training, clearly defined expectations, and giving an outline of His vision. He provided a great role model and He provided constant support for each leader.

Recruiting Leaders

> *"As they were going along the road, someone said to Him, 'I will follow You wherever You go.' And Jesus said to him, 'The foxes have holes and the birds of the air have nests, but the Son of Man has nowhere to lay His head.' And He said to another, 'Follow Me.' But he said, 'Lord, permit me first to go and bury my father.' But He said to him, 'Allow the dead to bury their own dead; but as for you, go and proclaim everywhere the kingdom of God.' Another also said, 'I will follow You, Lord; but first permit me to say good-bye to those at home.' But Jesus said to him, 'No one, after putting his hand to the plow and looking back, is fit for the kingdom of God.'"* (Luke 9:57-62)

Essential Leadership Characteristics to Look For

1. They must be saved. You will know them by their fruit not their confession (Matthew 7:15-23).

2. Must have demonstrated, in some capacity, faithful service.

3. They must be teachable and reliable (2 Timothy 2:2).

4. They must have demonstrated a consistent commitment to the ministry vision (they make meetings without having to be constantly reminded, they consistently complete tasks, they are open to accountability and work well with others) in the manner in which they serve and financially support church or para-church.

5. If they are going to lead members of the church or organization in ministry areas, they must have demonstrated some level of confidence in their ability to lead.

6. They must demonstrate a commitment to serve under leadership like Joshua did with Moses or Timothy was with Paul (John 21:15-17).

7. They must have a good reputation among the members of the church or from other organizations they have served in (Acts 16:1-6).

A Model Recruiting Process

1. Christ recruiting Peter:

   a. Christ healed Peter's mother-in-law (Luke 4:38-39).

   b. Christ picked Peter's boat and then gave him the best fishing he ever had as a businessman (Luke 5:1-11).

   c. Christ challenged Peter to do something for Him before He called Peter to serve Him.

   d. He then gave Peter and the other disciples the opportunity to observe His miracles (John 2) and his teachings (the Sermon on the Mount in Matthew 5-7).

   e. He then tested them. Christ was with them on the water (Matthew 8), sent them to minister on their own, then put them back on the water without him in the boat, and then came walking on the water (Matthew 14:22-31).

   f. He let Peter, James, and John experience the Mount of Transfiguration, and then the Garden of Gethsemane.

   g. He touched Peter in three areas: Personally. His daily life (Peters business Luke 5). Peter's commitment to Christ's Lordship in the worst times of his life.

   h. Christ accepted failure but still demanded a strong commitment to the ministry goals (John 21:15-17).

The Importance of a Clearly Defined Strategic Process

1. There must be a one paragraph vision and mission statement.

2. There must be ministry descriptions (same as job descriptions) for that particular ministry area so that the person taking over responsibilities clearly understands the mindset behind the leader's expectations.

3. In a church setting the area they serve in should be a place the members exercise their spiritual gift (1 Peter 4:10; Ephesians 4:16). This is the best fit because their service is empowered by the Holy Spirit (1 Corinthians 12:4-8; Ephesians 4:7).

4. There must be specifically defined goals and objectives. These may be one-year goals or three-to-five-year goals.

5. There should be an organizational chart that clearly defines the implementation of the vision statement.

6. Once anyone is appointed to a position, there should be regular meetings to provide answers to any concerns as well as training and coaching for ministry effectiveness.

Discipleship Training

Spiritual leadership is the development of relationships with the people of a Christian institution or body in such a way that individuals and the group are enabled to formulate and achieve biblically compatible goals that meet real needs. By their ethical influence, spiritual leaders serve to motivate and enable others to achieve what otherwise would never be achieved.

"Remember those who led you, who spoke the word of God to you; and considering the result of their conduct, imitate their faith." (Hebrews 13:7-8)

A. Biblical leadership is a life-to-life experience of accomplishing ministry objectives while at the same time changing lives for the glory of God (Mark 10:41-44).

B. Christ's walk with Peter before He released Peter to preach and lead the apostles.

1. His call was focused on developing a deep commitment to following His leadership (Luke 5:10-11; John 1:37). Following was attached to:

   a. Faith, trust, belief

   b. Cleave

   c. Obedience

   d. Self-denial

2. Jesus was always after a comprehensive disciple's program that required total commitment to God's divine will (Luke 6:22-23; 14:26-28; John 12:23-26).

3. Christ provided them on-the-job training (Luke 10:1-29).

4. Christ worked with Peter's failure (John 18:15; 21:15-17):

   a. Satan influenced Peter's decision making but Christ told Peter to get behind Him not away from Him (Matthew 16:21-23).

   b. Cut off the guard's ear.

   c. He denied Christ.

   d. Christ meets with Peter, challenging Peter's love for Him.

C. Bless Peter to achieve victory (Acts 2-3).

D. Was there to help Peter in difficult times (Acts 4).

A Summary Outline of a Training Process to Develop Ministry Gifts and Talents

A. Training Leaders to Understand Group Dynamics:

    1. There are stages in group development. The leader needs to be patient. There are as followers:

        a. Getting to know each other.

        b. Understanding the task.

        c. Developing a level of confidence in the leader.

        d. Developing confidence in the ability of each member of the committee.

        e. Develop a level of commitment to the accomplishment of the task.

        f. Achieving success in various parts of the task.

        g. Problem-solving.

        h. The group feeling a sense of accomplishment.

B. Process for Planning for Success:

    1. Planning for success must include these five major functions:

        a. Planning

        b. Organizing

        c. Directing

        d. Staffing

        e. Controlling

C. Motivating Workers to Work:

    1. If workers are stimulated to grow spiritually, this will become the motivating factor. Because their commitment to God em-

powers the process.

2. A leader that is always thinking positively and is excited about the project will encourage a workable attitude.

3. Give group members an opportunity to share ideas and be an active part of organizing the plan. This gives them ownership and stimulates a sense of responsibility.

4. The leader like Christ must concentrate more on the overall goal of the task rather than becoming easily upset by the problems of implementing the plan.

5. The leader should break up the task into small bites so that the group is motivated by the success experience. However, the project should not be divided into too many parts.

6. Leaders must take the time to encourage the workers.

7. Leaders should compliment workers for their dedication and their accomplishments.

   a. Specialized Training:

   • If they are leading a discipleship group, take them through the material and teach them small group dynamics.

   • If they are going to be a teacher, teach them to teach and test their learning by having them teach and then evaluate them. Put them in a group as a support teacher and then over time maturate them.

   • If they are going to lead a group let them work beside you and spend time explaining why you do what you do. Make sure they enjoy working with people and are patient to work with people even when they fail.

Conclusion

Delegating leadership responsibilities is critical for ministry development. The more opportunities members of a church or organization offer to gather and network, even as the church expands, the longer they will probably remain at the church or organization. The more people can become active in service, the longer they remain at the church or organization. Our availability in a busy world to work together and the shared accountability will increase the engagement and productivity of its members. Delegation leads to more efficiency and effectiveness for the expansion of a vision or organization. Delegation also creates a sense of ownership (this leads to a greater sense of responsibility for the church or organizations success) among those who lead and serve.

"You, therefore, my son, be strong in the grace that is in Christ Jesus. The things which you have heard from me in the presence of many witnesses, entrust these to faithful men who will be able to teach others also." (2 Timothy 2:1-2)

CHAPTER 10

Leadership Working Together to Create a Loving Church Environment

Introduction

Anytime someone serves and their major focus is only about getting the task done, their service is off center. The purpose of all service provided in the church is for *'the building up of body of Christ; until we all attain to the unity of the faith, and of the knowledge of the Son of God, to a mature man, to the measure of the stature which belongs to the fullness of Christ.'* (Ephesians 4:12b-13) This process then leads to a loving community *"...from whom the whole body, being fitted and held together by what every joint supplies, according to the proper working of each individual part, causes the growth of the body for the building up of itself in love."* (Ephesians 4:16)

The entire purpose of service in the local church is for the spiritual and emotional development of each member because the purpose for which the church exists is to *'present every man complete in Christ.'* (Colossians 1:28) This is because the mission of the church is to make disciples, create a loving community of believers (John 14:34-35), and to send them into the community and the world (Matthew 28:19-20; Acts 1:8).

The Mindset that Establishes a Loving Church Community

"A new commandment I give to you, that you love one another, even as I have loved you, that you also love one another. By this all men will know that you are My disciples, if you have love for one another." (John 13:34-35;)

Leaders loving God will love the People of God. A leader that makes the needs of members the focus for what they do is a leader who sincerely lives out the mind of Christ. *Therefore if there is any encouragement in Christ, if there is any consolation of love, if there is any fellowship of the Spirit, if any affection and compassion, make my joy complete by being of the same mind, maintaining the same love, united in spirit, intent on one purpose. Do nothing from selfishness or empty conceit, but with humility of mind regard one another as more important than yourselves; do not merely look out for your own personal interests, but also for the interests of others. Have this attitude in yourselves which was also in Christ Jesus..."* (Philippians 2:1-6)

A leader must first focus on falling in love with God (John 14:15; 15:4-5, 8, 10). This would cause them to serve based on God's strength not theirs (2 Corinthians 3:4-6; Colossians 1:29). When their focus is on Christ and what He directs them to do as a leader the outcome would be as follows:

1. The best way to focus on Christ while serving is to view His Word as everything (2 Timothy 3:17; 2 Peter 1:3-4).

2. Christ's emphasis with Peter and the others was to make them disciples by teaching them to keep His commands and therefore demonstrate their love for Him. After Peter denied Christ, Christ was more focused on Peter's love for Him more than Peter's service for Him (John 21:15-17).

3. Leaders' spiritual growth produces loving characteristics (Galatians 5:22-25).

4. A commitment to keep God's commands produces much fruit (John 15:5) creating a loving community. *"My Father is glorified by*

this, that you bear much fruit, and so prove to be My disciples. Just as the Father has loved Me, I have also loved you; abide in My love. If you keep My commandments, you will abide in My love; just as I have kept My Father's commandments and abide in His love." (John 15:8-11)

5. They would demonstrate grace for those who are weak because each leader is reminded that they live by grace (Ephesians 4:7).

6. Leadership would be based on the needs of others (1 John 3:16-17; 4:7-11). This kind of service blesses the church because it vividly demonstrates the love of God (Acts 9:36-43 — Tabitha's service to the widows).

7. Leaders that are committed to God bless their church membership (Acts 16:1-3).

8. Leaders functioning focused on glorifying God leads to Christ being lifted up (as they develop and demonstrate His character) which causes God to grow His church (Acts 2:42-47)

Without loving people, the church will have lost its value (1 Corinthians 13:3; Revelation 2:4) and Christ picks up His lampstand and leaves the church because one of His major character traits is love (1 John 4:7-14). Each ministry leader must serve the people in their ministry area by:

1. Regularly praying for them. If members of their committee are sick, at least call and send a card.

2. Keep up with birthdays and anniversaries.

3. The people in a leaders committee should not be people who just work for that ministry. They should, over a period of time, become an extension of your friendship.

Develop a Loving Community of Believers Through the Comfort and Care Ministry

"Now there are <u>varieties of gifts,</u> but the same Spirit. And there <u>are</u> varieties of ministries, and the same Lord. There are <u>varieties of</u> effects, but the same God who works all things in all persons. But to each one is given the manifestation of the Spirit <u>for the common good.</u>" (1 Corinthians 12:4-8)

Purpose

This ministry serves as a support to deacons as they seek to care for the needs of hurting members. The comfort and care givers will provide extended support for members who need continual support over a period of time.

The comfort and care Ministry will oversee the six vital areas: long-term illnesses, major illnesses, bereavement, comfort and care training, comfort and care givers who are hurting, as well as be fully supportive when family members of members have passed (it is sometimes difficult for deacons, elders, if the church has elders, to keep up, and the pastor to be at all the wakes and funerals of members whose <u>family members</u> have passed).

Ministry Objectives

1. Organize members to visit those who are in the hospital for long-term hospital care (1 Thessalonians 5:14-16).

2. Seek to be supportive to families who are caring for someone in long-term hospital care.

3. Find committed members who would visit the sick and shut in and minister to them.

4. Deacons should regularly provide the Lord's Supper to those who are sick and shut in.

5. Assist the pastor by being supportive to those individuals who are experiencing major illnesses.

6. Keep the pastor updated about what is taking place in this ministry.

7. Train potential (future) comfort and care givers.

8. Recruit members for the care ministry.

9. Must organize the ministry to support families at wakes, funeral services, and after the funeral services are completed. The following items will be foremost during these occasions:

   a. Represent the church leadership as designated by the pastor.

   b. Offer encouragement.

   c. Initiate calls, visits, and show concern for the family.

   d. Make sure Resolutions are written and read.

   e. Make sure flowers are sent to immediate family members of the deceased.

   f. Organize a card being sent to the family.

10. Serve families that are in the new membership ministry. These individuals mostly likely have not been assigned to a deacon. If a new member in the new membership ministry becomes ill, whether it is a short team or long-term illness, the comfort care ministry serves them until they are assigned to a deacon at the end of the new membership training.

Members Can Love Each Other Through the Ministries of the Church

"Pay close attention to yourself and to your teaching; persevere in these things, for as you do this you will ensure salvation both for yourself and for those who hear you." (1 Timothy 4:16)

1. Have greeters who, during worship, seek out new members or visitors and make them feel welcome.

2. Develop a caring community through Sunday school classes. This is where certain members in the class commit to keep up with those who become sick or may experience family emergencies.

3. Develop a caring community of believers through the women's, men's, singles, marriage, choir, and silver-star ministries. Birthdays and anniversaries can be highlighted. When someone is sick the ministry can seek to keep up with them.

4. Have the intercessory prayer ministry updating the leaders of the prayer needs of the church. They must also do follow-up to make sure to report prayers that are answered. This keeps leaders and the church community encouraged.

5. Develop church-wide fellowship activities such as:

   a. Church picnics.

   b. Family Night out — a night of fun activities.

   c. Fifth Sunday fellowships where there is fun and food for the entire family.

   d. Thanksgiving Feast.

   e. Fellowships geared to ministry to the young adults.

   f. Each Sunday encourage members to mingle and get to know each other.

Conclusion

The entire purpose for which God puts people in responsible positions in the church is to care for His flock. *"But we proved to be gentle among you, as a nursing mother tenderly cares for her own children. Having so fond an affection for you, we were well-pleased to impart to you not only the gospel of God but also our own lives, because you had become very dear to us."* (1 Thessalonians 2:7-8)

Leaders are responsible to grow God's people spiritually so as to not neglect them when they hurt, to stir them to worship, to cause them to want to become disciples of Christ, to hold them accountable when they sin, and to reach the lost. In the New Testament, a church that was faithful in serving God's people, by caring for His sheep, increased in number (Acts 6:7; 9:31).

> *"So, the church throughout all Judea and Galilee and Samaria enjoyed peace, being built up; and going on in the fear of the Lord and in the comfort of the Holy Spirit, it continued to increase."* (Acts 9:31)

CHAPTER 11

Staying Fit to Lead

Introduction

> *"I am the vine, you are the branches; he who abides in Me and I in
> him, he bears much fruit, for apart from me you can do nothing."*
> (John 15:5)

The spiritual development and influence of a leader is like water to the
body. Without water the body becomes dehydrated and the person
becomes weak and can eventually die. Without remaining spiritually
fit, leaders can become tired or lax in their leadership, thereby letting
the church become more of an organization than an organism, which
represents the body of Christ. Leaders experiencing ministry burnout
can become irritable, short tempered, and apathetic.

The spiritual influence of a leader also allows the church to become
better equipped to resist the attacks of Satan (Acts 20:28-31). If leaders
are not steadfast, sober, and alert, Satan will be provided the opportunity to devour us with this life's worries and cares (1 Peter 5:7-8).
*"Therefore, my beloved brethren, be steadfast, immovable, always abound-
ing in the work of the Lord, knowing that your toil is not in vain in the
Lord."* (1 Corinthians 15:58)

Recognizing and Addressing Ministry Burnout

One of the tragic paradoxes of burnout is that the people who tend to be the most dedicated, devoted, committed, responsible, highly motivated, better educated, enthusiastic, promising, and energetic suffer from burnout. Why? Partially because these individuals are idealistic and perfectionists. They expect too much of themselves as well as of others.

1. Definition:

    - Burnout is "a syndrome of emotional exhaustion, depersonalization, and reduced personal accomplishment that can occur among individuals who do 'people work' of some kind.

    - To them, ministry burnout is when people get to the point of just putting in their time, not making waves, and just barely getting by or going through the motions.

2. Personality Traits That Can Lead to Burnout:

    - Workaholic, perfectionist, not a people person or a people pleaser, High D personality, or don't like getting help. These traits can lead to high levels of frustration and stress and can even lead to bitterness and resentment. Serving God becomes an obligation.

    - Workaholics put in lots of time at work, then at church, collapsing on family so that family relationships become strained. This person can become more committed to finishing their task and lose sight of how what they are doing works to complement the overall church vision.

    - Perfectionists expect everything and everyone to work out meticulously perfect. Church or church people do not line up in straight lines so this personality trait can lead to stress and frustration.

    - Not a people person – Church ministry is first about healing broken people. This requires patience which this trait does not exhibit.

- People pleaser – This can be stressful because not everyone is going to be pleased with everything we do at all times.

  » High D personality – Church people expect to be served, not constantly told what to do.

  » Don't like getting help – "I don't need any help. I can do it myself. I know that everybody else thinks we should do this project a different way, but after all, I make the rules here."

  » A person that experienced conditional love from parents – This person only feels significant when what they do meets approval and is productive. This can become very stressful and, if approval is not met, the person can become bitter and resentful.

  » Setting goals too high and not meeting them can lead to continual stress that leads to burnout. This person is also someone who can take on too much responsibility.

3. Addressing Ministry Burnout:

   When there is hope and a daily dependency on the power of God through the work of the Holy Spirit and direction from His Word, generally speaking, ministry burnout can be prevented. However, there are steps we can take on a consistent basis to prevent it. I have divided them into several categories and if a person develops this into a normal way of living, they will be able to manage their stress and avoid the dreaded ministry burnout.

   - When we can actively maintain a lifestyle that allows us to be strong both physically and spiritually and sustain a sense of hope or positive expectancy. The positive use of adrenaline:

   - We must do our best not to function only on adrenaline. Rather, attach adrenaline to our call, which determines our goals and objectives. Take on new projects only if they are directly related to what the vision of the ministry determines and your spiritual gift.

- Evaluate carefully whether there are resources in place (or are they readily and properly accessible) to support the development of new projects.

- Take time off. This simple act will prevent days where you will experience depression because the adrenaline is gone and allow you to thoroughly rest when you are off.

- When you find that you are depending on adrenaline to keep you going, stop, get some rest, spend time with God, re-focus so that your life is focused on the strength that comes from the Spirit of God (2 Corinthians 3:3-5; Colossians 1:29; Philippians 4:13; John 14:25-27).

4. Stress management:

- Be willing to deal with past experiences that may have created bitterness and an unforgiving spirit.

- Delegate things that someone else can do.

- Take time off. Don't get involved in other things when you are supposed to be resting.

- You may try working on a project that is totally opposite to what you normally do so that you redirect some of your energy. This can be refreshing.

- Spend time with your spouse and do not allow the times of intimacy to be neglected.

- Be willing to share difficulties and painful things that maybe occurring in your life and ministry (James 5:16-18).

- Relax with articles or TV shows that will make you laugh.

- Get some exercise.

5. Learn the art of waiting on the Lord (Psalms 27:14; 40:1; Isaiah 30:18; 40:27-31). Learn to be patient (Galatians 5:22). Sometimes we make a request to God but become stressed as we wait on Him. Learning to wait is learning to trust God believing that *"all things work together for the good of those who love Him, those who are called according to His purposes."* (Romans 8:28). Key to this passage is for "those who love Him." Those who love Him keep His commandments (John 14:15). Waiting on God is to trust Him while we keep on obeying Him no matter the circumstances. A great example of this is Joseph in relation to being in jail twelve long years and David being mistreated by Saul for twelve long years.

- David said; *"I wait for the Lord, my soul does wait, And in His word do I hope."* (Psalms 130:5). *"Yet those who wait for the Lord will gain new strength; They will mount up with wings like eagles, they will run and not get tired, they will walk and not become weary."* (Isaiah 40:31)

- *"The Lord's lovingkindnesses indeed never cease, for His compassions never fail. They are new every morning; great is Your faithfulness. The Lord is my portion," says my soul, Therefore I have hope in Him." The Lord is good to those who wait for Him, to the person who seeks Him. It is good that he waits silently for the salvation of the Lord."* (Lamentations 3:22-26)

6. Managing your time based on points in Stress Management.

7. Avoid a perfectionist attitude.

8. Mental practices:

- When people hurt us, we can let that play over and over in our heads. Try not to focus on the past, especially when it leaves you feeling angry. Stay busy doing something completely different during these times.

- Focus on the present.

- Try to maintain your objectivity. Keep everything focused on your goals and objectives.

- Learn to say no.

- Remember your duties, be flexible, but remain on task without feeling a sense of guilt.

9. Cultivate a loving congregation (Discussed in chapter 10):

- Learn the passages of scriptures that teach how to respond to an enemy or persons that offend you and focus more on what God is teaching you to do rather than what they are doing to you.

- Treat everyone the same.

- Make few demands on them.

- Encourage members to have concern for each other (Matthew 22:36-40; John 13:34-35).

- Never harbor resentment.

> ## Remember this principle:
>
> ### DON'T LIVE UP TO PEOPLE'S EXPECTATIONS —ONLY GOD'S EXPECTATION (GALATIANS 1:10).

Steps to Remaining Spiritually Light

Do not neglect your family. There will always be a struggle between serving the needs of your family and church (1 Corinthians 7:32-35).

Do not allow the intimacy in your marriage to die (1 Peter 3:7). If we allow it, then we become ineffective for ministry.

Serve based on your spiritual gifts (Ephesians 4:1-7; 1 Peter 4:10-11).

This keeps you spiritually empowered which makes for less physical wear on you.

Make a point to be faithful in giving. It leads to righteousness because it requires faith (2 Corinthians 9:6-10).

Adopt some good spiritual habits:

1. Develop a consistent prayer life (Nehemiah 1:4-11; 1 Thessalonians 5:17).

2. Find a person committed to grow spiritually and live humbly before God and ask them to be your prayer and accountability partner (James 5:16-18).

3. Always view yourself as needing to grow (Philippians 3:7-16). As a result, you will do the following:

    a. Plan to make Bible study a habit for you and your family.

    b. Be a part of the church's spiritual grow structure.

    c. Keep these verses at the forefront of your mind:

       • *"Such confidence we have through Christ toward God. Not that we are adequate in ourselves to consider anything as coming from ourselves, but our adequacy is from God, who also made us adequate as servants of a new covenant, not of the letter but of the Spirit; for the letter kills, but the Spirit gives life."* (2 Corinthians 3:4-6)

       • *"...All Scripture is inspired by God and profitable for teaching, for reproof, for correction, for training in righteousness; so that the man of God may be adequate, equipped for every good work."* (2 Timothy 3:16-17)

    d. Don't allow yourself to get caught up always stressing on physical needs (Luke 12:21-31). I know this is hard (well, for me, it can be sometimes) but it is the best thing because if you allow this to control you it will become hard for you to serve God faithfully (Luke 8:14). Solve this by doing the following:

- *Fear God* (Psalm 112:1-3; 128). *Live conscious of God's presence daily.*

- *Be a good steward of whatever God has provided to you and your family* (1 Timothy 6:6-10).

- *Be a good giver* (Luke 6:38; 12:34).

- *Seek wisdom* (Proverbs 24:3-5).

"He humbled you and let you be hungry and fed you with manna which you did not know, nor did your fathers know, that He might make you understand that man does not live by bread alone, but man lives by everything that proceeds out of the mouth of the Lord." (Deuteronomy 8:3)

Live sensitive to the inner workings of the Spirit of God (Ephesians 3:16-17). The inner workings of the Holy Spirit are:

1. He is committed to us at the point of <u>salvation forever</u> (John 14:16-17).

2. He <u>convicts us</u> of sin (John 16:7-11).

3. He <u>reminds us</u> of God's Word (John 14:26).

4. He <u>illuminates the Word of God</u> for us to understand (1 Corinthians 2:10-15).

5. He <u>comforts us</u> in times of grief (John 14:6).

6. He <u>prays for us</u> when we are in pain and don't know how to pray (Romans 8:26).

7. He <u>provides fruit</u> that shapes our character when we choose to walk in the Spirit (Galatians 5:22-25).

8. He <u>guides us into a true understanding</u> of God's Word (John 16:13) so that we can live free from the influences of the flesh (John 8:31-32).

Things to remember as a leader:

1. Work with your ministry to make the church's vision a reality, don't just work (Habakkuk 2:1-4). Seeing God move in blessing your life and those around you can be strengthening. Assisting the church as it reaches certain milestones can be encouraging.

2. Be spiritual minded; what I mean by this is refrain from using common sense and always search the scriptures seeking the will of God (Deuteronomy 1:13-15; Colossians 3:1-4).

    a. Must maintain a commitment to the authority of scripture (Matthew 28:19-20; 5:17-20; 2 Peter 1:16-21; 2 Timothy 3:12-16; Colossians 1:9-11). This also reduces arguments and stimulates spiritual growth and a deeper understanding of God's Word when there are conflicts in the church.

    b. A leader's commitment to the authority of scripture must supersede their desire to maintain church traditions when those traditions violate the Word of God (Colossians 2:6-8; Matthew 15:2-9).

    c. We must not lean on our feelings to determine whether or not we obey the Word of God. By renewing our minds (whenever what you think is contradicted by scripture, adjust to what God's Word is saying) the Spirit of God sanctifies us so we are constantly moving from the flesh to the Spirit. By remaining in God's Word, we bear much fruit (John 15:1-11), we become true disciples of Christ, and our prayer life produces better results.

3. When you find people that may not like you or are purposefully difficult to deal with focus on loving them the way the Word of God directs you. This increases your prayer life and commitment to walk with God and therefore produces spiritual maturity (1 John 4:7-16).

4. When God challenges your common sense and forces you to trust Him for the results you desire, make a conscious choice to live by

faith and not by sight. God rewards those who live by faith (Hebrews 11:6).

"For this reason I bow my knees before the Father, from whom every family in heaven and on earth derives its name, that He would grant you, according to the riches of His glory, to be strengthened with power through His Spirit in the inner man, so that Christ may dwell in your hearts through faith; and that you, being rooted and grounded in love, may be able to comprehend with all the saints what is the breadth and length and height and depth, and to know the love of Christ which surpasses knowledge, that you may be filled up to all the fullness of God. Now to Him who is able to do far more abundantly beyond all that we ask or think, according to the power that works within us, to Him be the glory in the church and in Christ Jesus to all generations forever and ever. Amen." (Ephesians 3:14-21)

Conclusion

Leaders have a higher level of expectations in God's eyes. For instance, Moses was not allowed in the Promised Land because he disobeyed God. Another example given is the high accountability of teachers; they are to be judged more strictly (James 3:1). Discipleship is not achieved by just teaching believers. it takes place through observation as well (Matthew 28:20; Hebrews 13:7). As in a family in which a husband and wife are charged to create a culture that stimulates the development of their child (Proverbs 22:6), God's expectations of leaders are high. Leaders are tasked with transforming the lives of those they touch. In other words, each leader leads by influence; it is a life-to-life experience.

CHAPTER 12

Commitment Stimulates Great Leadership

Introduction

Leaders generally seem more committed to the title of their positions or how it impresses the congregation, rather than the core purpose for leadership (2 Thessalonians 2:1-8). The core purpose of leadership is to transfer the believer's current lifestyle to life of Christ (Philippians 1:23-25; 2 Corinthians 4:11-12). Each believer is led to experience the guiding light and love of Christ (Hebrews 13:7-8), the person we all come to worship. When the writer of Hebrews states that "Jesus is the same yesterday, today, and forever," he was not making a reference to the actual Jesus of yesterday. He is stating is that the leaders of chapter 2 lived with such a deep commitment to Christ, imitating His life each day, that the character of Christ lives on today. So as people grow to respect, trust, and follow their leaders, the Christ of yesterday works through them. As the leaders had come to reflect Jesus in their daily lives, they have paved the path to experience Him in a true and relevant way each day (Colossians 3:1-4). It is this commitment to be like Christ that shapes our commitment to the church (Hebrews 10:23-26).

The pivotal element that makes this a reality is the focus that Christ had when He developed leaders. Christ did not tell the disciples to go or disciple others until they were committed to be His disciples. Christ invested forty more days after His resurrection to ensure that they were ready to be His leaders for His glory.

The Bible consistently demonstrates a pattern of discipling believers in the expectation that eventually these believers will be mature enough to disciple others (2 Timothy 2:2). Examples of these patterns can be found in Elijah and Elisha, Moses and Joshua, Eli and Samuel, Christ and the disciples, Barnabas and Paul, Paul and Timothy and Titus. These individuals held a commitment to discipleship that led to productive, sustained results.

Once believers are discipled, the process for training them to be leaders may begin. This process intensifies because the expectations are higher (Acts 20; 1 Timothy 3:1-11) as compared to someone who has no desire to be a leader. The level of responsibility may also increase (Acts 15:1-5; 1 Timothy 4:11-16) for the trained leader based on the position they occupy.

Definition of Discipleship and Leadership

Discipleship

"Discipleship is that process of spiritual development which occurs in the framework of the accountable relationships of the local church whereby Christians are progressively brought from spiritual infancy to spiritual maturity and are to repeat the process with others" (written by Dr. Tony Evans).

Spiritual Leadership

"Spiritual leadership is the development of relationships with the people of a Christian institution or body in such a way that individuals and the group are enabled to formulate and achieve Biblically compatible goals that meet real needs. By their ethical influence, spiritual leaders serve to motivate and enable others to achieve what otherwise would never be achieved."

Discipleship Establishes Committed Leaders

Discipleship was always a call to learn and then to serve (Luke 5:1-11). The goal of training disciples of Christ was to develop a complete knowledge of the Word (Ephesians 3:17-19; Colossians 3:16-17; Acts 20:25-32), and to diligently obey it. When this is achieved, leaders faithfully:

1. Attend Bible study (John 14:15; 15:1-10) and worship (Acts 2:42-43).

2. Have a teachable spirit (2 Timothy 2:2).

3. Have a commitment to love others no matter who they are (Matthew 22:36-40). The church, as a result, is committed to caring for the hurting and helping the weak (1 Thessalonians 5:14-15).

4. When leaders remain spiritual minded (Acts 6:3; Deuteronomy 1:13-15), it makes circumstances easier to resolve objectively because each issue is guided and controlled by the Word of God, rather than opinions (Acts 15:1-22).

5. Discipleship stimulates a greater commitment to a Biblical approach to ministry, rather than a philosophical approach to ministry (Colossians 2:8-10).

A. A true disciple is committed to unconditionally sacrifice their lives for Christ (Matthew 10:37; Luke 14:26; Mark 3:31-35; Luke 9:59-62). To be a disciple means to be bound to Jesus and to do God's will (Matthew 12:46-50; Mark. 3:31-35). This means that during Jesus' earthly ministry the disciples had literally left everything to "follow" Him (Matthew 19:27-30). When a leader is a true disciple:

1. Sacrificing for Christ becomes second nature (Philippians 3:7-11). This establishes a higher involvement of leaders in the vision and mission of the church.

2. Leaders become faithful givers (Luke 12:29-34; Matthew 19:16-

30) because their commitment to the world diminishes (Matthew 6:19-24).

B. Leaders that are committed to discipleship become true models that members can emulate (1 Timothy 4:12; Hebrews 13:7-8). This leads to stronger:

1. Leaders in the home teaching men to be better husbands and fathers.

2. Single parents who model their growth in Christ as they raise their children.

3. The level of spiritual growth taking place in the church grows (1 Thessalonians 1:7-8).

C. Leaders that are true disciples become better followers (1 Corinthians 1:9; Matthew 16:21-23).

1. This spirit guides leaders to be more submissive to church leaders, thus creating more unity and harmony in the church (Hebrews 13:7, 15-17; 1 Thessalonians 1:2-5; 5:12-13).

Conclusion

"And we proclaim Him, admonishing every man and teaching every man with all wisdom, that we may present every man complete in Christ. And for this purpose also I labor, striving according to His power, which mightily works within me." (Colossians 1:28-29)

The discipling of a leader is more important than training someone to just complete a task. This is important because what a leader does affects the spiritual development of a believer (1 Timothy 4:16). The spiritual development of a believer leads to changes that affect their families, character, interpersonal relationships, jobs, and their involvement in community affairs. Believers make major decisions because of their commitment to Christ. As a result, leaders must be trained in an effective manner so that believers truly grow up into the fullness of Christ.

CHAPTER 13

A Biblical and Theological Definition of the Church

Introduction

The church throughout the years has been defined historically and philosophically, based on its lack of response or based on its response to the social problems in America — a social institution. This definition alludes to the church as a building, based on the various denominations, and based on its political power. However, there is a tremendous need to evaluate the Biblical and theological definition of the church. In this chapter, we seek to define the church based on a Biblical and theological analysis. This is by no means a comprehensive definition but, for the sake of this book, an overview.

An Overview of the Words for Church

There are several words, but I would like to examine the word used most frequently for church (*ekklesia*), by analyzing its Old Testament and its New Testament usage.

Old Testament Meaning

There are two Old Testament words used for an assembly and the act of assembling. They are (*qahal*) and (`*edah*). It is not so much a specification of the members of the assembly as a designation of the occurrence of assembling.

1. A general definition of the terms:

    a. `*edah* is the unambiguous and permanent term for the ceremonial community as a whole.

    b. *qahal* is the ceremonial expression for the assembly that results from the covenant, the Sinai community in the Deuteronomistic sense, and for the community in its present form.

2. The word "*qahal*" can refer to the following:

    a. A general assembly of the people (1 Kings 12:3)

    b. The assembling of the people including women and children (Jeremiah 44:15; Ezra 10:1; Nehemiah 8:2). (Secular meaning)

    c. The gathering of troops, and in Ezekiel it refers to nations other than Israel (Egypt, 17:17; Tyre, 27:27; Assyria, 32:22).

3. The word "`*edah*" refers to the following:

    a. When the term is used in Exodus 12:3 and suggests that the congregation of Israel first came into being with the command to celebrate the Passover and leave Egypt.

    b. The people gathering before the tent of meeting.

    c. It points to the community as centered in the cult or the law.

Of the two words "`*edah*" and "*qahal*," only "*qahal*" refers to the Greek word "*ekklesia*." This Greek word was most used by the apostle Paul.

New Testament Meaning

The word "*ekklesia*" is derived from the Greek word "*kuriakos*," which means "belonging to the Lord," and is only referred to twice in the Gospels, both times mentioned by Christ (Matthew 16:18; 18:17).

"*Ekklesia*" refers to the following:

1. Generally:

    a. It refers to a group of believers in a particular city where there can be several house churches. Paul writes his letters to these cities (1 Corinthians 1:2; 2 Corinthians 1:1; Galatians 1:2; 1 Thessalonians 1:1).

2. Specifically:

    a. It refers to the local church. This local church is viewed as the total community, the church.

    b. A group of believers in a local church is not regarded as a part of the whole church. Each church was viewed as representing the entire body of Christ.

3. Secular meaning:

    a. Refers simply to a gathering or assembly of persons, a meaning that is still to be found in Acts 19:32, 39, 41.

An Overview of the Biblical Definition of the New Testament Church

Who is the church?

1. Christ — He is the first to mention the word church (Matthew 16:18 universal church; Matthew 18:17 local church), and He is the head of it (Ephesians 1:22; Colossians 1:18). Since we are in Christ, we represent the church on earth for Christ, collectively and cooperatively (Romans 6:3-7; 1 Corinthians 3:16; 1 Corinthians 6:12-20). Judgment must first begin with the household of God (1 Peter 4:17).

2. All those who accept Christ into their lives are representatives of the church in society (Matthew 5:13-16; 1 Corinthians 3:16-23, Ephesians 3:16-17). The church does not exist for itself, but for its

impact on individuals, families, and communities (Matthew 28:19-20; Ephesians 3:10-11).

What is the church?

1. The church should be a viable process that impacts believer's lives, constantly stimulating growth (through the teaching, praying, fellowship, and evangelism; Acts 2:42-47) and commitment to Christ through His Word (1 Timothy 4:8).

2. The church should be an environment where the believers are constantly stimulated to submit every part of their lives to the authority of God (1 Timothy 3:15).

3. The church should impact a believer so that they are now able to impact society for the good.

4. The church represents and reflects the person and program of God in history (Luke 17:21).

5. The church must function in accordance with God's Word (1 Timothy 3:13; 1 Corinthians 14:40).

6. The church must not allow tradition to control its proper functioning (Colossians 2:8).

7. The church must move from programs to comprehensive ministries. It must seek to impact the whole man (Ephesians 4:11-13; Colossians 1:28).

8. The church must not be satisfied with mediocrity; it must always strive for excellence (Colossians 1:16-18; 1 Timothy 3:15). When this occurs, the church will prove itself effective in the market place.

Summary:

The New Testament local church represents a group of baptized believers of Jesus Christ (1 Corinthians 1:2; 12:12-14), working together to carry out His plans, purpose, and will (Ephesians 1:11). These believers must gather regularly (1 Corinthians 1:2; 11:18; Acts 20:7; Hebrew 10:24, 25) for the building up and equipping of one another (Ephesians 4:11-13; 1 Timothy 4:1-16) through the teaching, prayer, singing, Lord's supper, fellowship (Acts 2:42). This will be done as a result of the use of individual gifts (Romans 12:3-21; 1 Corinthians 12-14) so that believers will be imitators of Christ (Ephesians 4:1-2; 5:1-2) to be presented perfect in Him (Colossians 1:28-29). These believers must then become witnesses for Christ in the local community, and the world (Acts 2:42-47; 13:1-4).

The Goal and Purpose of the New Testament Church

If we do not operate on God's agenda, we would not experience God's results.

The Goal:

1. The main focus of the church is to make disciples (Matthew 28:19-20; Mark 16:15-16; Acts 1:6-11). This is the command. As a result, all church ministries, programs, and structures should be constantly scrutinized so that this process can occur. As Paul states in Colossians 1:28, his focus was to present everyone perfect in Christ.

    a. The above-mentioned goals will only be attained if the church must address sin (1 Corinthians 5:12-13). First as a result of members who hold each other accountable on an individual basis (Matthew 18:15-17). The church which holds each member accountable corporately (1 Corinthians 5). Also as a result of the church restoring those who have fallen into sin (Galatians 6:1-2).

    b. The church must also seek to maintain unity (Ephesians 2:14-22), by way of the Lord's supper in a Biblical manner (1 Cor. 11:27-32), fellowship, and worship.

c. The goal of the church is to become a nation unto itself (1 Peter 2:9-12). It will have its own:

- Government (Acts 20:27-35; 1 Timothy 3:1-11) for the care of its citizens (Ephesians 2:19).

- Court system (1 Corinthians 6:1-6).

- Accountability system for the effective development of the citizens (Matthew 18:15-20; 1 Corinthians 5; 2 Corinthians 2:1-10).

- Means of caring for those in need (Matthew 25:31-46).

d. The goal of the church is to keep Christ functioning practically in the community and world (Ephesians 1:22-23). As a result, it is the responsibility of the church to be a witness for Christ to the world (Acts 1:8).

The Purpose:

1. Israel's sole purpose was to be God's royal priesthood that would demonstrate His glory to the surrounding nations (Exodus 19:5-6).

2. This focus is the same for the New Testament church as found in Matthew 16:17 and Ephesians 3:10-11; 1 Peter 2:9-10.

3. The New Testament church must demonstrate the glory of God (1 Corinthians 10:31; Colossians15-17; Ephesians 5:20).

4. The purpose of the church is to be a community where "believers use their gifts to serve each other for the glory of God." (1 Peter 4:10; Romans 12:4-6; 1 Corinthians 12:21-31).

5. Even though believers once saved are established by God (Ephesians 1:3-4) to experience the fullness of God (Ephesians 3:16-21), it is only through the church that a believer can experience spiritual maturity (Ephesians 4:12-13). So the major focus of the church is to present believers complete in Christ (Colossians 1:28-29).

6. The purpose of the church is to demonstrate the love of God for those who come to church (1 Corinthians 13:3; Ephesians 4:16) and expose what that love means to the world (John 17:20-23).

7. The purpose of the church is to restrain the impact of Satan on the world (Matthew 16:17-19; Ephesians 3:10).

Biblical Images of the Church

The People of God:

This emphasizes God as being the one who chooses Old Testament and New Testament believers. God did not adopt a nation; he created His own nation through Abraham (Exodus 15:13,16; Numbers 14:8; Deuteronomy 32:9-10; Isaiah 62:4; Jeremiah 12:7-10; Hosea 1:9-10; 2:23). In the New Testament, he says:

1. *"There is no one righteous, not even one; there is no one who understands, no one who seeks God. All have turned away they have together become worthless; there is no one who does good not even one."* (Romans 3:11-12)

   a. *"For he chose us in Him before the creation of the world to be holy and blameless in His sight."* (Ephesians 1:4)

   b. *"But we are bound to give thanks to God always for you, brethren beloved by the Lord because God chose you from the beginning to be saved, through sanctification by the Spirit and belief in the truth. To this he called you through our gospel, so that you may obtain the glory of our Lord Jesus Christ."* (2 Thessalonian. 2:13-14; look at Ephesians 2:8-10; 1 Thessalonians 1:4)

   c. *"But you are a chosen people, a royal priesthood, a holy nation, a people belonging to God, that you may declare the praises of him who call you out of darkness into his wonderful light."* (1 Peter 2:9)

   d. Baptism is a sign that we are God's children (Romans 6:1-4).

There is a goal that God's people must set as their focus, and that is to be holy (Ephesians 1:4; 5:25-27; 1 Peter 1:13-16; 2:9).

The Body of Christ:

The image of the church as the body of Christ emphasizes that the church is the focus of Christ's activity now, just was his physical body during his earthly ministry. The image is used both of the church universally and of individual local congregations.

1. This illustration of the image of the church emphasizes how the church is interconnected with Christ as a collection of believers (Colossians 1:27; Galatians 2:20).

2. This is a result of the following:

    a. Christ is the head of the church (Colossians 1:18) and believers make the individual parts (Ephesians 2:14-18; 4:11-16).

    b. Believers, united with him, are being nourished through him, the head to which they are connected (Colossians 2:19). This image is virtually parallel to Jesus' image of himself as the vine to which believers, as the branches, are connected (John 15:1-11).

    c. The church is guided and controlled by his direction and his activity.

    d. 1 Corinthians 12 describes the gifts, which develops the concept of the interconnectedness of the body (Ephesians 4:16).

    e. Members of the body are to bear one another's burdens (Galatians 6:2) and restore those who are found to be in sin (VI).

    f. Members can be excommunicated from this body and therefore lose God's protection (Matthew 18:8,17; Romans 16:17; 1 Corinthians 5:12-13).

3. The body is also viewed as a group of believers who gather together for genuine fellowship (Acts 2:42; 1 Corinthians 12:26).

a. This does not mean merely a social interrelatedness, but an intimate feeling for and understanding of one another.

4. Because there is one head and one body, despite the diverse needs and gifts of members, the body must seek to be unified (1 Corinthians 12:12-13; Ephesians 4:4-6).

a. The lack of unity was aggressively discouraged by Paul to the Corinthian church (Romans 16:17-18; 1 Corinthians 1:10-17; 11:17-19).

5. The body of Christ is not just a local group of believers, but it extends itself as a universal church (Colossians 3:11; Romans 11:25-26,32; Galatians 3:28; Ephesians 2:15).

"I do not ask on behalf of these alone, but for those also who believe in Me through their word; that they may all be one; even as You, Father, are in Me and I in You, that they also may be in Us, so that the world may believe that You sent Me." (John 17:20-21; NASB)

The Temple of the Holy Spirit:

It is the Holy Spirit at Pentecost that brought the church into being. It is Christ who stated that the disciples will do greater things because of the ministry of the Holy Spirit (John 14:12).

1. The church whether it is individual or local is now indwelt by the Holy Spirit.

a. Individuals (1 Corinthians 3:16-17; 6:19; Ephesians 2:21-22)

2. The Holy Spirit also imparts His life to the church (Galatians 5:22-23).

a. The presence of such qualities is indicative of the activity of the Holy Spirit and thus, in a sense, of the genuineness of the church.

3. The Holy Spirit promised by Jesus Christ, is to come to give power to the church (John 16:7; Acts 1:8; 2:47).

4. It is the Holy Spirit that binds the body in unity before God. This is not uniformity but oneness in aim and action (Acts 4:32; 2:44-45).

5. The Holy Spirit develops sensitivity to the Lord's leading (Acts 10:11-48).

6. The Holy Spirit presence is evidence of the believer's salvation, and Christ being with believers (Romans 8:9-10).

7. The Holy Spirit will help illuminate the Word of God, and guide believers into all truth (John 14:26; 16:13; 1 Corinthians 2:10-15).

8. It is the Holy Spirit that dispenses the gifts to all believers (1 Corinthians 12:11).

9. It is the Holy Spirit that makes the church holy and pure (1 Corinthians 6:19-20).

   a. For just as the temple was a holy and sacred place under the old covenant because God dwelt in it, so also are believers sanctified under the new covenant because they are the temple of the Holy Spirit.

A Summary Review of the New Testament Church

The church mentioned by Christ on two separate occasions (Matthew 16:18; 18:17) was not referred to as an institution but an "*ekklesia*," meaning an assembly of individuals who He considered to belong directly to Him. In Matthew 16:18, Christ made reference to the universal church, but in Matthew 18:17, He made reference to a local assembling of believers. Paul follows Christ example when he refers to the church.

In Ephesians 5:23,25, Paul makes reference to the universal church but in 1 Corinthians 1:2, 4:17, and several other passages, Paul refers to the local church. Paul also states that there are four important principles that should characterize the universal and local church. They are faith, hope, and love with the greatest being love (1 Corinthians 13:3), as well as the Word of God which he states should dwell in believers richly (Colossians 3:15-17), and Jesus Christ, presented through the Word, must serve as the chief cornerstone (Ephesians 2:20).

Therefore, the New Testament local church represents a group of baptized believers of Jesus Christ (1 Corinthians 1:2; 12:12-14), working together to carry out His plans, purpose, and will (Ephesians 1:11). These believers are baptized because they have first, by faith, accepted as fact, that Christ died for their sins, and secondly have confessed Him as Lord (Romans 10:9,10; 1 Corinthians 1:17).

These believers must gather regularly (1 Corinthians 1:2; 11:18; Acts 20:7; Hebrews 10:24,25) for the building up, and equipping of one another (Ephesians 4:11-13; 1 Timothy 4:1-16) through teaching, prayer, singing, Lord's Supper, fellowship (Acts 2:42). This will be done as a result of the use of individual gifts (Romans 12:3-21; 1 Corinthians 12-14; 1 Peter 4:10) so that believers will be imitators of Christ (Ephesians 4:1-2; 5:1-2) to be presented perfect in Him (Colossians 1:28-29). These believers must also become witnesses for Christ in the local community, and the world (Acts 1:8; 2:42-47; 13:1-4). They must also seek to function as one body, united in Christ, characterized as a loving community, for God's glory (Acts 2:44-47; Ephesians 2:14-18).

Finally, the absolute foundation for developing church ministry must rest on the authority of the Word of God (2 Timothy 3:16; Matthew 4:4; Acts 20:27), and the goal of its ministry must be to disciple (Matthew 28:19-20) believers to be mature in Christ (Colossians 1:28-29). The church must also bear the responsibility of representing Christ comprehensively before the community (Ephesians 1:22).

Summary Implications

A. The church is not to be conceived of primarily as a sociological phenomenon, but as a divinely established institution. Accordingly, its essence is to be determined not from an analysis of its activity, but from scripture.

B. The church exists because of its relationship to the Triune God. It exists to carry out its Lord's will by the power of the Holy Spirit.

C. The church is the continuation of the Lord's presence and ministry in the world.

D. The church is to be a fellowship of regenerate believers who display the spiritual qualities of their Lord. Purity and devotion are to be emphasized.

E. While the church is a divine creation, it is made up of imperfect human beings. It will not reach perfect sanctification or glorification until its Lord's return. (Quoted from "Christian Theology" by Millard J. Erickson, page 1049)

Achieving a unified cohesive church is no easy task. There are different personalities and backgrounds, whether academic, socio-economic, or cultural. Sometimes differences exist because people go from church to church and are trained by each church to think a certain way doctrinally, based leadership styles or on how ministry should operate philosophically. Similar difference existed in Christ's day which caused Pharisees, Sadducees, the elders, high priests, or Zealots to constantly attack Christ. Rabbinical teachings also affected how the disciples thought at times, believing that Christ while on earth was going to reestablish the Davidic throne (Mark 10:32-44). The major issue with all of this is the glory of God would not be manifested without unity; *"I do not ask on behalf of these alone, but for those also who believe in Me through their word; that they may all be one; even as You, Father, are in Me and I in You, that they also may be in Us, so that the world may believe that You sent Me."* (John 17:20-21; NASB)

The Lord has done much to make sure that the church, which is the body of Christ and the only thing the kingdom of God is committed to (Ephesians 1:22-23), has all it needs to be great. The Trinity is engaged for the purpose of making it great; *"Now there are varieties of gifts, but the same Spirit. And there are varieties of ministries, and the same Lord. There are varieties of effects, but the same God who works all things in all persons. But to each one is given the manifestation of the Spirit for the common good.* (1 Corinthians 12:4-7; NASB) This is so important that Paul would continue to say that until this process is engaged dynamically for Christ, we truly will not experience what the church is all about. *"Now you are Christ's body, and individually members of it."* (1 Corinthians 12:27).

The Godhead's involvement does make Christ's body productive but it also, because of this process, creates a cohesive assembly that at its core is God's instrument of love. This means that the manner in which it operates would be unifying. *"There is one body and one Spirit, just as also you were called in one hope of your calling; one Lord, one faith, one baptism, one God and Father of all who is over all and through all and in all. But to each one of us grace was given according to the measure of Christ's gift."* (Ephesians 4:4-7; NASB) This is achieved when believers are committed to grow spiritually by making the church a viable organism for Christ. When this is each believer's focus, *"from whom the whole body, being fitted and held together by what every joint supplies, according to the proper working of each individual part, causes the growth of the body for the building up of itself in love."* (Ephesians 4:16; NASB) This is why when spiritual growth is not taking place the church becomes dysfunctional. *"Now the deeds of the flesh are evident, which are: immorality, impurity, sensuality, idolatry, sorcery, enmities, strife, jealousy, outbursts of anger, disputes, dissensions, factions, envying, drunkenness, carousing, and things like these, of which I forewarn you, just as I have forewarned you, that those who practice such things will not inherit the kingdom of God."* (Galatians 5:19-22; NASB)

Notice the above passage concludes with *"will not inherit the kingdom of God."* Paul explains to us in Ephesians what the kingdom of God is in Ephesians 1:13-14. *"In Him, you also, after listening to the message of truth, the gospel of your salvation — having also believed, you were sealed in Him with the Holy Spirit of promise, who is given as a pledge of our inheritance, with a view to the redemption of God's own possession, to the praise of His glory."* (NASB)

Until we make this process a major focus, Christ is not glorified; He is not lifted up before the world (John 12:32). We would seem just like the world, full of division and factions and therefore not as powerful as the church is designed to be. Drawing people to Christ would not be as effective. Transforming lives would not as dynamic. Therefore, the church would have a difficult time moving from conflict to harmony.

Moving from conflict to harmony is a process that is meticulously outlined by the Word of God which must always serve as the authority over the church (the Word also provides the leadership structure and accountable process that serves to shape how conflict should be resolved). This allows Christ to be the head of the church, not just because the Word of God says so, but because it is functionally taking place in the church being applied with all wisdom especially since *"it is adequate, equipped for every good work."* (2 Timothy 3:17). When the scriptures remain as the authority, everyone is accountable, and as their spiritual growth serves to help them understand the scriptures, the Word of God creates an objective process that directs everyone to progressively move from conflict to harmony. This is what is modeled for us in Acts 15 that empowered the spread of the Gospel throughout the world.